THE ASSASSINATIONS OF JOHN AND ROBERT KENNEDY

For Anita

CONTENTS

The End Is the Beginning 1

From Dunganstown to Blackett Strait 6

The Name of the Game Is Politics 18

Senator from Massachusetts 25

Winning the Big One 34

Two Crises 45

Death in Dallas 56

A Nation Mourns 64

Oswald — Was He the Only One? 75

Enter Marguerite and Marina 84

Puzzles and Contradictions 95

Senator from New York 106

The Kennedys and Vietnam 115

In the Running 123

A Second Death, a Second Slayer 131

Epilogue: The Search Must Go On 140

Postscript: Into the 1990's 143

The End
Is the Beginning

Just below the Custis-Lee Mansion at Arlington, Virginia, lies a well-tended burial ground. There, at Arlington National Cemetery, near Washington, D.C., two brothers are buried. One is John Fitzgerald Kennedy, thirty-fifth president of the United States. The other is Robert Francis Kennedy, U.S. senator from New York at his death.

A low white picket fence surrounds the two graves. Above President Kennedy's resting place burns a gas-fueled Eternal Flame. The scene is peaceful, still, even though tens of thousands of visitors come here every year.

It was Mrs. John Kennedy who first suggested Arlington. In 1962, the year before the president's death, she asked, "Where will we be buried when we die, Jack?"

"Hyannis, I guess. We'll all be there," he replied.

1

(Hyannisport, Massachusetts, is still the Kennedy family's summer place.)

"Well, I don't think you should be buried in Hyannis. I think you should be buried in Arlington. You belong to all the people."

Most Americans make the pilgrimage to the Kennedy burial ground because they are devoted to an image and an ideal. The image is of two youthful men — the president died when he was forty-six, the senator when he was forty-two. Both were ruggedly handsome, lean, athletic, good at golf, sailing, and their favorite sport, touch football.

Both men were also husbands and fathers. John Kennedy, husband of the former Jacqueline Bouvier, had a daughter and a son. Robert Kennedy, who married Ethel Skakel, was the father of ten children (an eleventh was born after his death).

Adding to their image was that John Kennedy became the first U.S. president who was Roman Catholic. As a presidential candidate, and with Robert Kennedy as his campaign manager, he worked hard to overcome voter resistance to his religious faith. With the support of many millions of non-Catholic voters he won the 1960 election. President Kennedy proved that a candidate's religion need be no barrier to the highest political office in the United States.

A musical called *Camelot*, about the legendary King Arthur and his court, was playing on Broadway when John Kennedy entered the White House. Like King Arthur and his queen, the Kennedys lived graciously and joyously. Mrs. Kennedy (the press and the public always called her "Jackie") redecorated the somewhat neglected White House with beautiful American antiques and authentic reproductions. A White House tour became a great art experience. The presidential couple gave many lavish parties on their own for writers, artists, and musicians, as well as the required state dinners for foreign dignitaries. Washington became to many a second Camelot.

Of course, Robert Kennedy, who served as attorney general in his brother's cabinet, and his family had free run of the White House. The two brothers were close. One knew how the other thought and what his conclusions would be. They loved and respected each other and, just as important, they understood each other. Each by himself was a strong leader. Together they made an extremely effective team.

John Kennedy wanted his brother to follow him as president. In fact, right after his nomination he gave his brother a small gold case inscribed, "After I'm through, how about you?"

President Kennedy was assassinated in Dallas, Texas, on November 22, 1963. In office for little more than a thousand days, he had been on a political tour of Texas cities. The president's accused slayer, Lee Harvey Oswald, was himself killed two days later. Oswald's assassin, Jack Ruby, shot him as he was being transferred from one jail to another.

The nation's grief over the president's death began to transform the Kennedy image into the Kennedy ideal. The public forgot his human faults and started to regard him as a folk hero, almost a demigod. They enshrined him in Camelot.

At John Kennedy's death, Vice President Lyndon B. Johnson became president. Robert Kennedy continued to serve as attorney general for several months. In 1964 he resigned and ran for U.S. senator from the state of New York. He won. Four years later he decided to seek the Democratic nomination for president.

In the spring of 1968, Robert Kennedy entered the primary campaigns in several states. The California race was his first triumph. On June 4–5, the night of his California victory, he was in a Los Angeles hotel, celebrating with his campaign workers. A killer, Sirhan Sirhan, was waiting for him. The second Kennedy died a day later of bullet wounds — and took his place beside his brother in Camelot. The transformation from image to ideal was complete.

But even cherished ideals have a tendency to fade and disappear in time. Camelot might now be remembered only as a storybook castle and a muscial title. Safely dead, the Kennedys might have taken their proper and undisturbed places in U.S. history textbooks.

But John and Robert Kennedy are not yet safely dead and buried; they will not be until the complete stories of their assassinations are known. It's been pretty well decided that Lee Harvey Oswald was guilty of the murder of the president, and Sirhan Sirhan of the murder of Senator Kennedy. But were they solely guilty?

Did each act alone, or did they also have help, accomplices? Was there a conspiracy behind each crime — two or more people who schemed and acted together? Could there have been larger networks of killers involved?

The judgment at first was that Oswald and Sirhan each committed his crime for his own private, twisted reasons. Now, however, hints increase that suggest something more. The motives for the two slayings might not have arisen solely from the tortured thoughts and emotions of Oswald and Sirhan. There might have been political reasons as well. The slayings might involve people in high places, some still alive.

At present there is no positive proof, but the controversy mounts. John Kennedy liked to quote an old Chinese proverb: "The journey of a thousand miles begins with a single step." The journey to find the truth about the Kennedy slayings is longer than a thousand miles, larger than the dimensions of this book.

Let us take that first step.

From Dunganstown to Blackett Strait

To know the Kennedys, you must know a little about the history and traditions of Ireland. You must also know something of the Irish beginnings in America. For the Kennedys, American from head to toe, were also shaped and molded by their Irish ancestors — just as every other American (starting with the Native American) is influenced by his old world heritage.

For centuries in Ireland, most of the Irish people were the oppressed tenant farmers of the English landowners. Poor, uneducated, they raised grain for their landlords and lived mainly on the potatoes that grew abundantly in their cottage gardens.

Despite their poverty, the Irish were always a proud people. They kept alive the ancient stories of Irish kings and heroes, they sang their lovely old songs, and they frolicked often to celebrate a harvest or a wedding.

And they passionately loved their rainy green island, with its blue lakes and grass-covered hills. Some Irishmen served abroad with the British army, some settled in foreign lands, but Ireland was always home to them. They forgot its poverty and remembered only its beauty.

There were always Irish patriots who fought to free their country from British rule. Like John and Robert Kennedy, many were doomed to die young while serving their native land.

In the mid-1840's disaster fell upon Ireland. A blight struck the potato crop, and the people's food supply was just about wiped out. Thousands starved to death; many of the living roamed the countryside in search of something to eat. In those days there was no emergency famine relief from other countries. Even the English landowners turned their backs on the stricken Irish.

Those who had saved a little money determined to leave their ancestral home. Among the emigrants was Patrick Kennedy, twenty-five years old, of Dunganstown, County Wexford, in the southeast corner of Ireland.

Patrick sailed from the nearby port of New Ross, in a vessel bound for Boston. The six-week voyage was a nightmare. The ship was small, and the sea was rough. The passengers were jammed below deck, with no room even to stand up straight. Food and water were scarce. Almost all the thousands who fled Ireland during the potato famine went through this same agony.

Patrick Kennedy survived for a time. He landed in Boston, found work as a cooper (a barrel-maker), and became part of a fast-growing, prospering city. He married Bridget Murphy, fathered three daughters and a son, and died at thirty-five, victim of the dreaded disease cholera.

His son, named Patrick Joseph, was only a year old when his father died. He attended a parochial (church-operated) grammar school, and as a teenager began working on the East Boston docks. But this Patrick Kennedy was different from most of the other dockworkers. He did not drink, he saved his money, and he planned his future. He bought one saloon, then another, and in time became a power in the whiskey business.

Patrick Kennedy also became a power in Boston politics. Staying in the background, he helped organize the new Irish voters in their fight against the old-line Yankee political machines. In 1887 he married Mary Hickey. Next year their first child was born, a boy christened Joseph Patrick.

Joseph Patrick Kennedy — Joe Kennedy to the millions who knew him as an immensely rich businessman, government official, and statesman — got off to a running start. Most other Irish-American children of his day attended parochial school. Joe's father enrolled him at Boston Latin School, where the offspring of the best New England Yankee families had been educated for generations. Boston Latin, then and now, demanded much from its students. Joe did himself and his family proud.

At graduation, Joe did not enroll at Boston College or Holy Cross, the choice of most college-bound Boston Irish students. He entered Harvard, where the competition was keener. A Harvard degree also meant a greater chance for success after college. Joe Kennedy was aiming high.

After being graduated from Harvard in 1912, Joe Kennedy became a state bank examiner. Moving fast, he soon became president of a bank — at twenty-five, the youngest bank president in Massachusetts. In 1914 he married Rose Fitzgerald, daughter of John F. ("Honey Fitz") Fitzgerald, longtime mayor of Boston.

Honey Fitz was well known for his renditions of "Sweet Adeline" and even better known for his tight control of Boston politics. His family was at the top rung of Boston's Irish Catholic social world. Rose herself was both beautiful and smart. She and Joe Kennedy were well matched. They settled down in a house in suburban Brookline. Rose began to raise a family, and Joe began to make his fortune.

Their first child was Joe, Jr. Then came John (until he became president everyone called him Jack), Rosemary, Kathleen (called Kick), Eunice, Patricia, Robert (called Bob or Robbie by his family and friends — the press called him Bobby), Jean, and Edward (called Ted or Teddy).

The elder Kennedy's money multiplied many times in the 1920's and 1930's. Stocks, real estate, imported Scotch whisky, the movie industry — he moved from success to success. Shortly before the 1929 stock market crash, he sold off his stock holdings — and thus had millions to use in buying stock bargains in the 1930's.

Joe Kennedy worked hard for his money. He and Rose worked just as hard to raise a good family. They wanted their children to grow up tall and strong, in body and mind. But Joe and Rose didn't want them to be concerned about money. So the parents set up a trust fund of more than a million dollars for each child (the values of the funds have since increased vastly).

With their finances taken care of, the sons and daughters would be free to work for the public good. The boys were aimed toward politics, the girls toward social service. "Never be second best," their father coached them. He was obsessed with winning.

In the late 1920's the Kennedy family moved from Brookline to the Riverdale section of New York City, then to the nearby suburb of Bronxville. Joe, Jr., and Jack were sent to boarding school. Choate, in Connecticut, was the school finally settled on. Joe, Jr., a good athlete and good student, made the teams and the honor roll. Jack was smaller and less of a scholar. He was enthusiastic about sports, but not about studies.

10

The family spent winter vacations at Palm Beach, Florida, and summers at Hyannisport, on Cape Cod. The children were forever swimming, sailing, playing touch football. Joe, Jr., was the natural leader. He and Jack were always fighting. The two were really good friends, but Joe was bigger and stronger. He usually won.

Joe and Jack were the first and second of the nine children. Bob, born eight years after Jack, was the seventh. "The first time I remember meeting Bob," President Kennedy recalled, "was when he was three and a half, one summer on the Cape." It was easy to ignore a little brother, but Bob — stubborn and determined — eventually made Joe and Jack know he was there.

Jack followed Joe into Harvard. Joe made the football team, but Jack was too light. Jack did make the swimming team, however. He developed into a fine swimmer, a skill that was to serve him well in World War II. He became a better student, too. But at the time, campus politics held no interest for him. Neither did national and world politics, which were coming to a boil in the middle and late 1930's.

At the end of 1937, President Franklin D. Roosevelt appointed the senior Joseph Kennedy ambassador to Britain. Kennedy had already held important government posts under President Roosevelt, but this was the highest honor he had been granted. People smiled when they heard that an

Irish-American — whose forefathers had suffered severely under the English — was now ambassador to Britain.

In the spring of his junior year Jack got Harvard's permission to serve as his father's secretary in London. Jack took notes, traveled across troubled Europe, and saw the clash that was about to take place. His interest in world affairs was aroused.

Back at Harvard Jack expanded his notes into a senior thesis, which helped him to be graduated *cum laude* ("with honors"). After graduation he turned the thesis into a book, called *Why England Slept*. It was published in 1940.

Jack said the book was "more *work* than I've ever done in my life." The book was a well-balanced analysis of why Britain had not prepared for World War II, which had begun in 1939. Ambassador Kennedy was gloomy about Britain's chances in the struggle. He strongly advised President Roosevelt to keep America out of the war, saying that Germany was sure to win. In 1940 he resigned his post and came home.

Joe, Jr., and Jack were certain their country would be involved in the war. In 1941, well before Pearl Harbor, they were commissioned as naval officers. Joe was in the Navy's air arm, Jack in administrative work. But Jack did not want to remain a desk-bound officer, even though he had barely passed the Navy's physical exams. In college he had injured his back playing football, and had qualified for the Navy only by taking months of back-strengthening exercises.

Jack wanted duty that would use his skills as a small-boat sailor, skills acquired during his Cape Cod summers. So he applied for the MTB (Motor Torpedo Boat) School at Melville, Rhode Island.

These PT (patrol torpedo) boats were swift craft that could reach speeds of about forty knots (about fifty land miles an hour). Eighty feet long, they were armed with .50-caliber machine guns and 20-millimeter cannon. They also carried four torpedoes for launching against enemy ships.

The crew of a PT boat consisted of two officers and eight or nine enlisted men. All had to be young, hardy, and adventuresome, for PT warfare was a most dangerous game. PT boats were used for lightning strikes at much bigger ships and enemy shore installations. They saw action in virtually all the waters of war, but achieved their most spectacular successes in the South Pacific.

That's where young Lieutenant (junior grade) Jack Kennedy was sent — to the PT base at Tulagi in the South Solomon Islands. The base was near Guadalcanal, which the U.S. Marines had recaptured in a long and bloody struggle.

Mister Kennedy (all naval officers below the rank of lieutenant commander are called "Mister" when spoken to) was soon given command of *PT-109*. He and his new crew soon put the boat into first-class shape and were ready for action.

Action was soon forthcoming. The PT squadron

was now operating out of newly freed Rendova. On August 1, 1943, *PT-109* was making its twentieth combat patrol. On several previous patrols it had exchanged fire with the enemy. On this night *PT-109* — along with fourteen other PT boats — was setting up a blockade in Blackett Strait. Purpose of the blockade: to surprise and trap Japanese ships coming through the strait.

At two o'clock in the morning the destroyer *Amagiri* and several sister ships were sailing north through the strait, returning to their base at Rabaul. Spotting the blockade, the Japanese vessels revved up to flank speed and began firing. *PT-109*, with Mister Kennedy at the helm, closed in, hoping to launch a torpedo.

But *PT-109*'s engines failed to respond quickly. Instead, the *Amagiri* rammed the boat, cutting it in half. Kennedy was knocked away from the helm. He landed on his bad back, injuring it painfully. One crewman, McMahon, was severely burned by the explosion of the gasoline tank. Two others were missing and never found.

At dawn Mister Kennedy and his crew were still in the water, hanging onto the bow section of the boat. They took a vote: swim to a nearby Japanese-held island and surrender; or swim to a farther, uninhabited island and take their chances. The second choice was unanimous.

The executive officer, Ensign Thom, and an extra officer, Ensign Ross (aboard only for the one night), led the swim. Mister Kennedy held the life-

14

jacket strings of the badly burned McMahon in his teeth and towed the sailor to the island. The swim took more than five hours, Kennedy's back injury knifing at him all the way.

The ordeal was by no means over. The crew was still in danger. They were exhausted and hungry. Kennedy was determined to lead them to safety. He spent all that night in the water, hoping to signal a passing PT boat. He detailed Mister Ross to do the same on the following night. Still no luck. Next day he shifted his men to what seemed to be a better-located island. Then he moved them to a third island, Nauru, where they found food left behind by the Japanese.

The crew had been sighted after that first night by friendly islanders. They reported the Americans' position to a New Zealand infantry patrol on the island of New Georgia. In a short time the *PT-109* men were rescued.

Jack Kennedy returned to stateside naval hospitals for treatment of his old back injury, made worse by the *Amagiri* ramming. He had also contracted malaria, and his weight fell to 125 pounds — skin and bones on his six-foot frame. When he was awarded the Purple Heart for his injuries and the Navy and Marine Corps medal for his heroism, his photos showed a gaunt and ravaged man. His medal citation said, "His courage, endurance, and excellent leadership contributed to the saving of several lives . . ."

In the middle of 1944, Kennedy, now a Lieutenant, senior grade, entered Chelsea Naval Hospital, near Boston, for treatment. He was well enough to spend weekends at Hyannisport with his family. There, on August 2, the Kennedys got word that Joe, Jr., was missing in action.

Joe had volunteered for a danger-filled mission — to destroy Nazi submarine pens on the Belgian coast. He took off from an English air base in a plane loaded with explosives. Joe intended to fly close to the pens, then bail out. The plane was to go ahead by remote control and crash into the pens. But the plane itself exploded before Joe had a chance to jump clear.

A month later tragedy again struck the Kennedy family. Jack's sister Kathleen (Kick) had met a British nobleman, the Marquess of Hartington, when Joseph Kennedy was ambassador. The two had been married only a few months before Hartington was killed fighting in France. Kick herself died in an airplane crash in 1948.

Nor were the wartime tragedies the first to take place in the Kennedy family. Rosemary, the eldest daughter, early on showed signs of mental retardation. She lived and traveled with the Kennedy family for many years, but eventually was sent to an institution in Wisconsin.

Bob, eighteen, was in a naval training program at the time of Joe's death. At once he asked for sea duty. He was soon assigned to the crew of the new destroyer *Lt. Joseph P. Kennedy, Jr.* But World War II was nearly over before the ship completed its shakedown cruises, and Bob saw no action.

At the start of 1945, Jack Kennedy — wasted and slowly recovering from back surgery — was separated from active naval service. That spring he was a newspaper correspondent at the first meetings of the new United Nations in San Francisco. That summer he covered the British elections in London.

A reporter's job, however, failed to capture his attention. As World War II ended in August, 1945, Jack Kennedy wasn't all that clear about his future.

The Name of the Game Is Politics

Ambassador Kennedy had great plans for his family, especially for his sons, and most especially in a political career for his oldest son. But when Joe, Jr. died the father did not lay his hand on Jack's shoulder and say, "Carry on in Joe's name" — or some such dramatic talk. Jack was left to find his future. He found it in politics.

In his forceful way the ambassador had always preached the advantages of a political career to his sons. A Kennedy could make his greatest contribution to the world as a politician, he said. It was the best way to win recognition and respect. And a political career would make maximum use of a Kennedy's talent.

Jack was somewhat leery of his father's preaching. He liked what a politician did after he won office — administering, legislating, making policies, and so on. But he wondered how he would like the job of running for office, of trying to get elected. He wasn't sure of his ability to meet the voters, to ring doorbells, to go through the grind, sweat, and exhaustion of a political campaign.

He was, however, the grandson of Mayor Honey Fitz and of politico Pat Kennedy. He was the son of a man who had enjoyed high government appointments. So Jack Kennedy decided to give politics a try.

The Democratic nomination for U.S. representative from the Eleventh Massachusetts Congressional District was up for grabs. Jack Kennedy, twenty-eight years old in the fall of 1945, set out to win it. The primary election, in which the candidates from the different parties were chosen, was to be held in June, 1946. The general election was to take place the following November.

When Jack Kennedy made up his mind to run, he showed the same resourcefulness and energy as he had earlier displayed as skipper of the *PT-109*. The Eleventh District sprawled over the slummiest parts of Boston and the most aristocratic parts of Cambridge, where Harvard University is located. Kennedy worked for votes all over the district.

He was thin as paper, and his skin was still yellow from atabrine, taken for his malaria, but he was out campaigning every day from early morning to late evening. He walked into saloons, stores, factories, firehouses, everywhere that people gath-

19

ered, shaking hands, telling what he could and would do for the voters.

Money was no problem. The Kennedy family fortune backed his efforts. It paid for newspaper and radio ads, billboards, posters, leaflets, and coffee meetings. But money was no substitute for hard work. Kennedy enlisted his old school and navy friends in the campaign. His helpers considered it an honor to wear a *PT-109* tie clasp. Bob, now a Harvard student, hustled for votes in Cambridge. Jack even put his mother and sisters to work.

In June, Jack Kennedy won the Democratic nomination. He beat the runner-up by a two-to-one margin. The November election was a shoo-in. No Republican candidate had won in the Eleventh District in many years.

In January, 1947, Jack Kennedy, now twenty-nine, took his seat in the first postwar Congress. (Another freshman congressman was Richard Nixon of California. He, too, had been a Navy officer who served in the Pacific.)

Kennedy served three two-year terms, 1947–53, in the U.S. House of Representatives. Harry S Truman was president, and the young Massachusetts congressman followed his lead in most national problems. Kennedy was a member of the House Labor and Education Committee, where he fought for liberalized labor laws.

He also fought for government aid to build new houses, especially for war veterans. This was opposed by the American Legion, largest of the veterans' organizations. The Legion wanted the government to pay a cash bonus to World War II veterans. Kennedy's anger at the Legion mounted. Finally, in a congressional debate he said, "The American Legion has not had a constructive thought for the benefit of this country since 1918!"

His defiance of the Legion paid off. Congress eventually passed a good housing bill.

Kennedy split with President Truman many times on foreign affairs. He disagreed with the President's reasons for involving the United States in the Korean War. Kennedy instead wanted his country to help Western Europe build up its defenses against Communism.

But he was always learning. In 1951, with Bob and their sister Patricia, Kennedy took a trip around the world. On the way, they had a good look at the Middle East. Later he voted for aid to this area of the globe. In a House of Representatives speech he said, "Many of us now feel that the United States has concentrated its attention too much on Western Europe."

By this time Bob was finished with college and law school. As a Harvard undergraduate, Bob had made the football squad as an end. But he had never played in enough games to earn his letter. Now he was a senior, and it was the last game of the season, the game against Yale. Bob was still on the bench. To make it worse, his leg was injured, all bandaged and taped. In the last minutes

21

of the game, Yale was ahead, 31–21. No hope for Harvard.

The coach decided to send Bob in for one play so he could earn his letter. Harvard was kicking off, and the kicker had instructions not to boot onto Bob's side of the field. But the kick misfired. The ball was picked up by a Yale halfback who headed straight for Bob. Young Kennedy just grinned and crashed into the runner, ending up under a pile of tacklers. Then, still grinning, he hobbled back to the bench.

Before he completed law school at the University of Virginia, Bob married Ethel Skakel, daughter of a wealthy Connecticut family. Their first child, a girl, was named Kathleen Hartigan, after Bob's sister who had died in a plane crash. Their second, a boy, was called Joseph Patrick III, after Bob's father and older brother.

By 1950 the House of Representatives was growing too small for Jack Kennedy. He was a little frog, only one of 435 House members, in a big puddle. He wanted to be a bigger frog in a smaller but more important puddle.

Kennedy had his choice of two such frog-and-puddle combinations. He could run for governor of the state of Massachusetts, or he could run for U.S. senator from Massachusetts. To win either one, he had to make himself known throughout the state.

So for two years Kennedy worked to earn a state-wide name. He flew up from Washington every

Thursday afternoon and spent the long weekend crisscrossing the state. He spoke at civic club luncheons, union meetings, church gatherings, anywhere he could find an audience. The strenuous schedule intensified the pain in his bad back. At the end of a hard day, a board under his mattress and a hot tub helped to ease the pain.

The campaign brought results. By 1952 everybody in Massachusetts knew Jack Kennedy. But in that year his road to the governor's mansion was blocked off. The popular Democratic Governor, Paul Dever, decided to run again. Nobody, however, was ready to oppose the equally popular U.S. Senator, Henry Cabot Lodge, Jr., Republican, who was also going to run again. Nobody, that is, except John F. Kennedy.

Lodge had been in office since 1936, taking time out for World War II service. He seemed unbeatable. Rich, aristocratic, handsome, he had strong Republican support. His father, Henry Cabot Lodge, Sr., had also served several terms in the U.S. Senate. In 1916 Honey Fitz had challenged the senior Lodge for his Senate seat. Cabot, Sr., beat John Kennedy's grandfather badly. Would Cabot, Jr., do the same to Honey Fitz's grandson?

The entire Kennedy family set out to win the election. Bob served as campaign manager, assisted by Teddy, now twenty years old. Patricia, Eunice, and Jean presided at countless coffee hours for Jack. Rose Kennedy held many formal receptions, attended by an estimated 50,000 Massachusetts women. They shook hands with Congressman Kennedy, admired Rose Kennedy's gown, and took tea and cookies. Then they went home and told friends and neighbors what a delightful experience it had been.

Joe Kennedy was everywhere behind the scenes. He talked to campaign workers, men of influence, public relations experts. He wanted to shape Jack's strategy and make him take a conservative stand on most issues. On one occasion he ran into one of Jack's liberal supporters. The elder Kennedy shouted at him, "You and your friends are trying to ruin my son's career!"

Later this supporter asked Jack, "How do you explain your father?" Joe Kennedy's son replied, "Just love of family." Then he modified his answer, "No. Pride of family." The real truth was that Jack Kennedy was running his own campaign and his own career.

In 1952 the presidential race was between Republican Dwight D. Eisenhower and Democrat Adlai Stevenson. In winning the presidency, Eisenhower beat Stevenson in Massachusetts by 208,800 votes. But Kennedy won the Senate seat, beating Lodge by more than 70,000 votes. In a Republican year, Democrat Jack Kennedy was the clear winner.

Honey Fitz was revenged.

Senator from Massachusetts

John F. Kennedy served in the U.S. Senate from 1953 to 1961. During those eight years a number of important things happened to him. He got married. He became involved with Senator Joe Mc-Carthy. His back problem brought him close to death. He was awarded a Pulitzer Prize. And he was elected president of the United States.

At thirty-six, Kennedy was young for a U.S. senator. But as a bachelor he was getting on in years. In 1953 he married lovely Jacqueline Lee Bouvier, who had attended Vassar College and the Sorbonne in Paris. The two had met when she was working as an inquiring photographer for the Washington *Times-Herald*. Jackie did her best to keep up with the sports-loving Kennedy clan — until she broke her ankle. Thereafter she cheered from the sidelines.

Jacqueline Kennedy was a quiet woman, but a strong one. She did not compete with her husband. Instead she worked with him: as his hostess, as his interior decorator, as his French and Spanish translator, as his wife and the mother of their two children, Caroline and John. Their relationship was deep and close.

At first Kennedy considered that his main duty as senator was to take care of Massachusetts. He pushed for laws and rulings that would help the state's industry: textile and shoe manufacturing, fishing, shipbuilding. To serve the state's voters better, he added extra staff members, paying them out of his own pocket. He spent most weekends in Massachusetts, where he listened to requests and problems.

Gradually Kennedy became drawn into wider responsibilities. One of these tasks was to decide what to do about Senator Joseph R. McCarthy, Republican of Wisconsin. McCarthy, chairman of the Government Operations Committee, had for years been hurling reckless charges about Communists in the federal government, especially in the State Department. Kennedy, a low-ranking member of this committee, was faced with a decision: was McCarthy right or wrong? Were there actually enough Communists holding government jobs to endanger the United States?

McCarthy continued to hold hundreds of hearings, investigations, inquiries. With his unproved accusations, he frightened the State Department into firing many innocent staff members. He saw Communists everywhere.

Kennedy's attitude toward McCarthy was complicated by many factors. Old Joe Kennedy knew and liked McCarthy. So did Bob Kennedy. He had been a staff lawyer on McCarthy's committee for many months, resigning only because of quarrels with McCarthy's chief assistants. Massachusetts voters liked McCarthy as a foe of communism. They excused his methods because they agreed with his goals.

But Jack Kennedy did not let "like" or "dislike" affect his thinking. His only question was, "Is McCarthy breaking the law by his Communist-hunting tactics?" While he was trying to decide, a resolution was proposed in the Senate. It read: "*Resolved*, That the conduct of the senator from Wisconsin is unbecoming a Member of the United States Senate, is contrary to senatorial traditions, and tends to bring the Senate into disrepute, and such conduct is hereby condemned."

The polite language of this resolution of censure did not hide its meaning. It said that McCarthy had disgraced the Senate and himself. Kennedy listened to the debate over the censure resolution and became pretty sure that he was in favor of it. In the end, however, Kennedy never voted on the resolution.

Before the debate ended, Kennedy was in the hospital. His back trouble, originally brought on by a football injury and complicated by his perilous *PT-109* adventures, was causing agonizing pain. He had suffered a similar, death-threatening attack during his 1951 world tour. Bob and Patricia stood by him in an Okinawa hospital for many days.

Now he had to submit to a spinal fusion operation. Before the operation, his adrenal glands were working poorly as a result of his wartime ordeal. After the operation they worked scarcely at all. Twice he came close to dying, so close that a priest said the last rites of his religion over him. Both times he recovered.

For months Kennedy was out of touch with the Senate. When the time came to vote on the censure resolution, he was still in the hospital. He might have had one of his staff register his vote for him. He didn't, because he had not heard the last part of the debate, and felt he was not prepared to vote.

Over the next several years, many critics took potshots at him for his failure to vote. Leftist critics said he was pro-McCarthy. Rightist critics said he was anti-McCarthy. Both sides charged him with being afraid to take a stand. Many said he should have shown "less profile and more courage."

The remark came from the title of John F. Kennedy's famous book *Profiles in Courage*. The book was begun as he lay recovering from his operation. For a long time he was bedded in a darkened hospital room or later in his father's Palm Beach house. His back still pained him sorely, but his mind was restless and active. He turned to a writing project on which he had earlier made many notes.

The project began as a magazine article and ended as a book. It was about U.S. senators and representatives who had followed their consciences instead of voter demands or pressures from fellow legislators. Thus it was about political heroes, men of courage, and so the title of the book.

Kennedy had plenty of advice and research assistance on *Profiles of Courage*. He sounded out historians and university professors. His chief aide, Ted Sorensen, dug up reams of source material. The Library of Congress sent him hundreds of background texts. Kennedy himself did all the writing and rewriting. After the book became popular, several critics accused Kennedy of having hired a ghostwriter. Kennedy was able to present ample proof that he alone was the author.

Profiles in Courage sold widely, and all over the world, too. It was translated into many languages. The book was awarded the Pulitzer Prize for biography in 1957. Long before the award was granted, the book helped Kennedy win a national name. People respect a politician who is also a serious author. A special version for young readers was even published.

In fact, *Profiles in Courage* did much to put Kennedy in the running for his party's nomination as vice president in 1956. He very nearly secured the nomination, losing to Senator Estes Kefauver of Tennessee in a close vote.

Later, Kennedy was glad that he'd lost the vice-presidential nomination. In 1956 Adlai Stevenson was running for the second time as the Democratic presidential candidate. He lost for the second time to Republican Dwight D. Eisenhower. Kennedy would also have been tagged as a loser.

Moreover, Kennedy's Roman Catholic religion might have taken a share of the blame for the Democratic loss. In 1956 the United States was not yet ready for a Roman Catholic on the national ticket. In 1960 much careful work went into preparing the country to accept such a presidential candidate.

After the 1956 convention, a friend tried to soften Kennedy's loss by telling him, "You're sure to get the vice-presidential nomination in 1960." His reply: "I'm not running for vice president next time. I'm running for president." That was Joe Kennedy's son speaking. His goal was now the top — and he was already on his way.

For example, he sent Bob Kennedy to travel with the 1956 Stevenson campaign party. Bob followed the Democratic candidate for weeks. He noted the mistakes Stevenson made, especially where he did not cooperate with the press. Stevenson fussed over his speeches until it was too late to make advance copies for the reporters. In 1960 Kennedy did not repeat Stevenson's mistakes.

During the years between 1956 and 1960 Kennedy followed the same plan he had used in running for Congress. He took every minute he could spare from his job as U.S. senator to work on the job of winning the presidential nomination.

At first Kennedy traveled mainly on commercial planes for his speechmaking tours. He also flew in hired private planes, big and little, with professional and sometimes very amateur pilots. The risks decreased when the Kennedy family bought a Convair (named *Caroline*, after Kennedy's small daughter) in 1959. Chief staffer Ted Sorensen was Kennedy's constant companion on these trips.

Of course, Kennedy did not deliver a brand-new speech to each audience. He and Sorensen kept a speech file on the plane. They selected parts from old speeches and combined them with new paragraphs to make a new-sounding speech. The two also turned out magazine articles that appeared in leading journals under the senator's name.

Speeches, articles, and interviews brought Kennedy to the attention of millions of Americans. They knew about his father, about *PT-109*, about his record in Congress. And they knew about his Catholicism.

The religious issue came up early and often, and Kennedy faced it squarely. The U.S. Constitution keeps politics and religion separated, and that was the way Kennedy wanted it, too. His Catholicism was a private matter, he said, and would have no influence on his decisions as president. At the same time he cut away from other Catholics who let their faith affect their politics.

Quite naturally John Kennedy was kidded about the political favors his father's money might be buying for him. At the 1958 annual dinner of the Washington Gridiron Club, a skit portrayed him singing — to the tune of "My Heart Belongs to Daddy" — a song that ran, "Just sent the bill to Daddy."

In his own speech later at the same dinner, Kennedy said he'd just received a telegram from Joe Kennedy that read, "Dear Jack: Don't buy a single vote more than is necessary. I'll be damned if I'm going to pay for a landslide."

As 1960 grew closer, Kennedy's campaign committee expanded. Brothers-in-law Steve Smith (Jean's husband) and Sargent Shriver (Eunice's husband) came to work for him. Larry O'Brien and Ken O'Donnell, old Boston friends, joined the staff. (The press called the staff the Irish Mafia.) Pierre Salinger, later his presidential press secretary, became campaign press secretary. Bob Kennedy took the full-time job of campaign manager.

Bob had spent the previous three years as chief counsel for the Senate Rackets Committee. His main job was to go after Jimmy Hoffa, president of the 1,700,000-member Teamsters' Union. The Rackets Committee hearings were televised, and Bob faced dozens of tough union thugs and sharp union lawyers while the TV cameras hummed. "It was like playing Notre Dame every day," Bob later recalled. Yet he shrugged off the many veiled threats to kill him.

Bob's savage pursuit of Hoffa helped earn him the reputation of being "ruthless." As Rackets Committee counsel, Bob was not able to bring Hoffa to trial. Later, as attorney general, he continued to chase the labor leader. Finally, in 1964, Hoffa was found guilty of bribing a jury. His appeals postponed imprisonment until 1967. Hoffa's eight-year sentence was later reduced by President Richard Nixon. Some years later Hoffa disappeared. He was believed to have been kidnapped and murdered. His body has not been found.

One of Bob Kennedy's abilities was a superb talent for organization. He laid out the campaign like a general planning a battle. Every staffer got clear-cut assignments and responsibilities. Key coworkers were lined up in all the states. Bob himself was at the center — everything channeled through him. And here he may have added to his reputation for ruthlessness. He would allow nothing to stand in the way of John Kennedy's march to the White House.

John Kennedy was relying heavily on his brother when he made his formal statement on January 2, 1960: "I am today announcing my candidacy for the presidency of the United States."

Winning the Big One

How does a presidential hopeful win his party's nomination? He gets the nomination by winning a majority of the delegate votes at the party's national convention. And how does he earn these votes? Most nomination-seekers campaign for them in several of the state presidential primary elections. Then they maneuver for more votes in the states they didn't campaign in.

Not all presidential hopefuls enter the state primaries, and virtually none runs in all of them. The number they enter depends partly on their campaign funds, partly on their chances of winning in that state.

Money was no problem to John Kennedy. Winning the state was the only consideration. And winning depended on who his opponent would be, how effective his own years of speechmaking in the state had been, how many influential friends he had made in the state.

In early 1960 Kennedy made his state primary choices: New Hampshire, Wisconsin, Indiana, West Virginia, Nebraska, Massachusetts, Maryland, and Oregon. No other candidate entered so many primaries that year. Kennedy felt he needed the backing of voters in all these states in order to win the nomination, and he had the money to campaign in them.

Two primaries were especially important: Wisconsin and West Virginia. In both, Senator Hubert Humphrey was his main opponent. Humphrey was really dangerous in Wisconsin, because he represented Minnesota, Wisconsin's neighbor to the west. It was almost like fighting Humphrey on his home ground. Humphrey had been Minnesota's able Senator since 1948, and he had been a good spokesman for all the upper Midwest.

Besides, Wisconsin was mainly Protestant and rural, although it had its share of Catholics and a few good-sized cities. The odds seemed to be against Kennedy. Nevertheless he tramped the streets of Wisconsin towns from the Upper Peninsula to the Illinois border. Again his sisters helped with coffee hours in Wisconsin homes, and his staff steered him to the political leaders in each community.

Kennedy took much flak from the press and from Humphrey spokesmen about his friends, his money, even his personal life. But he stuck to the business of campaigning. He discussed Wisconsin problems — rivers and forests, farm cooperatives, the St. Lawrence Seaway.

And when the votes were counted, Kennedy had won by a margin of fifty-six percent. He was able to claim two thirds of the state's convention delegates. He had spent no more money in Wisconsin than Humphrey did. His hard-slugging, dawn-to-midnight campaigning won the winning votes, many of them from Protestants, many from farm families.

In West Virginia an early poll predicted a sixty-forty landslide for Humphrey. That state was ninety-five percent Protestant, mostly rural. Experts were sure that a Boston Catholic had no chance in West Virginia.

At the time, West Virginia had many problems. Its people were perhaps the poorest in the country. A number of its coal mines, the state's biggest employers, had shut down. Others had fired most of their miners and turned to automation. Once-flourishing mining communities were now ghost towns. Strip mining, unchecked, had ruined great stretches of farmland. Many West Virginians were on welfare.

With Jacqueline beside him, Kennedy spoke in just about every town in the state. When he lost his voice, Teddy Kennedy or Ted Sorensen filled in for him. West Virginia's poverty affected him deeply, and his speeches were filled with passion and sympathy.

Much help in the West Virginia campaign came from Franklin D. Roosevelt, Jr. He was the son of the president whose New Deal in the 1930's gave substantial aid to the state. Kennedy battled the religious issue again, saying, "I am not the Catholic candidate for president. I do not speak for the Catholic Church on issues of public policy, and no one in that church speaks for me. . . ."

When that statement failed to end attacks, Kennedy went on television with FDR, Jr., answering tough questions that Roosevelt put to him. He said that as president

> [I] would not take orders from any pope, cardinal, bishop, or priest, nor would they try to give me orders. . . . If any pope attempted to influence me as President, I would have to tell him it was completely improper. . . . If I took orders from the pope, I would be breaking my oath of office . . . and commit a sin against God. . . . I would be subject to impeachment and should be impeached.

John Kennedy did his work well in West Virginia. He won sixty-one percent of the vote and carried forty-eight of the fifty-five counties. He won the black vote and the white Protestant vote. Facing such strength, Hubert Humphrey dropped out.

The 1960 Democratic convention was held in Los Angeles in July. Kennedy set up headquarters in the Biltmore Hotel, laying claim to a winning number of delegates. His claim was not dead certain, for delegates were free to change their minds as the convention progressed. Kennedy volunteers camped close to each of the state delegations and kept tabs on the voting trends.

Even though they had entered no primaries, strong contenders were hoping to get the party's nod. The most important were Adlai Stevenson of Illinois, twice a candidate and still a threat; Lyndon Johnson of Texas, Senate Majority Leader and widely known; and Stuart Symington of Missouri, veteran senator and former Air Force Secretary.

Before the voting started there was talk of deals, of putting up one of these men for president and letting Kennedy run for vice president. Joe Kennedy answered the rumors bluntly: "Not for chalk, money, or marbles will we take second place."

Kennedy won on the first ballot. As the roll was called by states, his score kept mounting. When West Virginia voted he had 750 of the 761 needed to win. Wyoming, next in order, had fifteen votes. Teddy Kennedy was there to see that Wyoming cast all fifteen for his brother, putting him over the top.

The first thing Kennedy did was to call Jacqueline, at home in Hyannisport awaiting the birth of John, Jr. Next, he thanked the delegates in a short speech. Third, he ate a midnight supper and went to bed. Fourth, he woke up the next morning and chose a vice-presidential running mate.

The man selected was Lyndon B. Johnson, who had presidential ambitions himself. Johnson was chosen largely because he could help get Kennedy votes in the South.

Not all the Kennedy staff approved of the choice. Johnson was very different from Kennedy. He was said to be a wheeler-dealer in politics, an off-again on-again friend, a deadly man to cross. Bob Kennedy was especially hostile toward Johnson. This hostility never really subsided.

The Republicans put up Richard M. Nixon as their candidate. Nixon was far better known than Kennedy. He had been vice president for eight years under Eisenhower, often acting as the president's hatchet man. He had one advantage over Kennedy which he himself never made use of — but which his supporters did. He was a Protestant.

As always, John Kennedy was a hard-driving campaigner. He crisscrossed the country in the *Caroline*, speaking everywhere. His talks were short, factual, and to the point. That point was: "It is time to get this country moving again." By that he meant the United States had become bogged down in the 1950's. It was losing its place as the world's leader.

Kennedy was a cool, unemotional speaker. He had a strong Boston accent and a trick of poking out his hand, palm down and at right angles to his audience, to emphasize his points. Some friends urged him to put more passion and pepper into his talks. Poet Robert Frost told him: "Be more Irish and less Harvard." But he never changed his style, and he never had to grope for words.

It was this low-key, controlled performance that may have won him the presidency. His control was demonstrated in four nationally televised "debates" with Richard Nixon. Not real debates, they were statements and responses by each speaker, plus questions put to them by a panel.

Nixon, for all his skill as a debater and all his experience on TV, came out a loser. For one thing, his appearance was bad. He looked pale and sweaty. His heavy beard stubble was covered by a thick layer of white powder, and both stubble and powder showed. He stuttered; his sentences were sometimes confusing; and he often failed to make his point.

By contrast, Kennedy looked good — tanned, healthy, alive. He spoke in short, crisp sentences, and his conclusions were clear as crystal.

This was the first time that all America saw the two candidates meet face to face. Many Nixon supporters and many on the fence switched over to Kennedy. He seemed to be the more likeable person. More important, he seemed to be the clearer thinker, the man to trust in a crisis.

Lyndon Johnson's campaigning in the South helped greatly. Johnson was the grandson of a Confederate soldier. He was also a strong advocate of civil rights. He brought the old and the new South into the Kennedy camp.

Most of the blacks in both the North and South hesitated about backing either Nixon or Kennedy. Then Dr. Martin Luther King, Jr., Baptist minister and black leader, fell afoul of the law. He was sentenced to four months at hard labor in a Georgia prison. The charge: no Georgia driver's license. The charge, of course, was only an excuse for punishing King for his civil rights activities.

At once John Kennedy called King's pregnant wife, Coretta, and promised to do all he could. Bob Kennedy called a Georgia judge, who ordered that King be released from this unjust sentence.

Kennedy's action swung most of the black voters to his side. Nixon had the same chance to help King, but he chose not to take it. His failure lost him millions of black votes.

The religious issue would not die, especially in the South. Kennedy made up his mind to explain, once and for all, and let this explanation stand for the rest of the campaign. To the Houston, Texas, Ministerial Association, he talked of "not what kind of church I believe in, for that should be important only to me, but what kind of America I believe in." He went on:

I believe in an America where the separation of church and state is absolute — where no Catholic prelate would tell the President (should he be Catholic) how to act, and no Protestant minister would tell his parishioners for whom to vote — where no church or church school is granted any public funds or any political preference . . . an America that is officially neither Catholic, Protestant, or Jewish. . . .

Even after this speech the religion attacks went on. But Kennedy had laid his position on the line for all to see. Many, but not all, of the once-doubtful voters were now convinced that Kennedy's private faith would have no influence on his public acts.

Nearly 69 million voters turned out on Election Day, 1960. In the South the vote was heavy. In the big cities it was light. The race was neck-and-neck. When the votes were totaled, Kennedy had won by a margin of less than 120,000. His Electoral College score was respectable, 303 to 219, but a shift of only a few thousand votes in a few key states would have cost him the election.

Wide margin or narrow, Kennedy was the winner. Between Election Day, November 8, and Inauguration Day, January 20, he prepared to take on the most important job in the world.

During those ten weeks Kennedy had to select a cabinet and fill about 1,200 other government posts. He had to formulate goals and programs to reach those goals. He had to set up policies on taxation, trade, defense, health, welfare, education, business and industry, transportation — and all the other matters that the federal government is involved in.

John Kennedy considered Bob for several cabinet posts and finally appointed him attorney general, head of the Justice Department. Ted Sorensen later reported: "Bob did not like it when the president joked at a post-inaugural dinner that he saw no harm in naming him attorney general to 'give him a little experience before he goes out to practice law.' "

Despite pressures, the president-elect remained relaxed and easy. On Thanksgiving Night, John, Jr., was born, a younger brother for Caroline.

One Sunday morning in December an ugly and ominous incident took place. A man named Richard P. Pavlick parked his car — loaded with seven dynamite sticks — in front of the Kennedys' Palm Beach house. Waiting for John Kennedy to drive to church, he intended to ram Kennedy's car and explode the dynamite. Pavlick changed his mind when Jacqueline and Caroline came to the door to bid Kennedy good-bye. He decided he didn't want to kill Kennedy in front of his family.

The Secret Service knew that Pavlick had threatened Kennedy earlier. They did not know that he was in Palm Beach until a few days after that Sunday incident. He was immediately arrested. A note found in his pocket "explained" why he was ready to kill Kennedy — and himself: "I believe that the Kennedys bought the presidency and the *Whitehouse* and until he really became president it was my intention to remove him in the only way it was available to me."

John Kennedy was asked later if he worried about being assassinated. He replied, "I guess there is always the possibility, but that is what the Secret Service is for . . . I guess that is one of the less desirable aspects of the job."

On January 20, 1961, John Fitzgerald Kennedy was sworn in as the thirty-fifth president of the United States. At forty-three he was the youngest elected president. (Vice President Theodore Roosevelt had been forty-two when he succeeded the assassinated President William McKinley in 1901.)

Bareheaded, on a bright, cold, windy day, John Kennedy took the oath of office. In his inaugural address he asked the nation and the world to put aside their differences and work together. Near the end of the speech he issued his now-famous challenges:

"And so, my fellow Americans, ask not what your country can do for you; ask what you can do for your country.

"My fellow citizens of the world, ask not what America will do for you, but what together we can do for the freedom of man."

With these words, the thousand days of the Kennedy Administration began.

Two Crises

Right from the beginning of Kennedy's presidency, crises kept shooting up all over the world. The United States was involved in most of them. Two such crises, one with Cuba alone, the other with Cuba and the Soviet Union, are important for at least two reasons:

1) They threatened to drag the United States into full-scale wars.

2) Critics now see a strong link between these crises and the death of John Kennedy, and perhaps also of Robert Kennedy.

Years before Kennedy became president, Fidel Castro started the revolution that led him to power in Cuba. Kennedy knew what Castro was up to. He wrote that Castro had "betrayed the ideals of the Cuban revolution" and had transformed Cuba "into a hostile and militant Communist satellite."

45

After the revolution, a number of anti-Castro Cubans escaped from the island. Many of them settled in Miami, Florida, and most of them were ready to become U.S. citizens. Others were eager to return to Cuba and destroy Castro. In the last year of President Eisenhower's term, the Central Intelligence Agency (CIA) began helping these people prepare to go back.

The CIA set up a training camp in Guatemala. There more than a thousand anti-Castro Cubans learned invasion and guerrilla warfare tactics. The plan was to land these fighters on Cuban shores from their own ships and under cover of their own planes. Once ashore, they were to scatter into the countryside and organize rebel bands among the peasants. They were to foment another revolution in the army and overthrow Castro.

The whole operation was to be conducted in such secrecy the world would never know the United States government was involved. The Cuban exiles were to take all responsibility. The plan was already well advanced when Kennedy first learned of it.

Kennedy was new in the presidency and he was inclined to take the word of experts. No high U.S. official was critical of the invasion plan — everyone was for it, including the CIA and the Armed Forces' highest command, the Joint Chiefs of Staff.

Somewhat suspicious, Kennedy nevertheless let

the preparations go on. He said later, "You always assume that the military and intelligence people have some secret skill not available to ordinary mortals."

A landing site in Cuba was chosen: the Bay of Pigs. Kennedy, still wary, didn't call a halt. His own Secretary of State, Dean Rusk, and his Secretary of Defense, Robert McNamara — and their staffs — urged him to give the invaders the green light. Kennedy finally said "Go!"

Sometime during the middle of April, 1961, about 1,400 men in seven small ships attempted a landing on the beaches of the Bay of Pigs. Castro's forces were ready for them. The invaders' air cover was destroyed. Their ammunition ship was sunk. The invaders themselves were slain or taken prisoner.

The whole operation had been botched. And soon the whole world knew the invasion attempt had been engineered by the United States. Kennedy realized there was no way to deny it. He told Lyndon Johnson: ". . . when I accepted the responsibility for this operation, I took the entire responsibility on myself. I think we should have no sort of passing of the buck or backbiting, however justified."

The clamor of criticism did not die down for a long time. Newspapers in the United States and around the world branded Kennedy as an unfit and incapable president. Demonstrations broke out in many cities. Protestors picketed the White House.

The Bay of Pigs disaster taught Kennedy a sharp lesson. Never again would he accept the word of an "expert" without thorough cross-checking. Never again would he allow the United States to be caught before the world in a lie. Never again would he risk the lives of brave men — in this case, the Cuban invaders — without seeing that they were properly trained and equipped.

However, Kennedy never got around to setting up a good system for checking on the CIA's undercover operations. In 1975 the CIA's involvement in the assassinations of foreign leaders came to light. Did the CIA scheme to eliminate Castro backfire? Or did Cuba's CIA act first — and eliminate Kennedy?

If the United States was humiliated before the whole world by the Bay of Pigs disaster, it regained its good name by its conduct in the Cuban missile crisis. The word "Cuban" is misleading. The real crisis was not with Cuba but with the Soviet Union.

The crisis lasted thirteen days, from October 16 to 28, 1962. When it began, it seemed highly possible that much of the world might be destroyed in a nuclear war between the United States and Soviet Russia. When it was over, reason had prevailed, and no nuclear missile had been launched.

There was still no real peace, but a fearful conflict had been avoided.

Here's what took place during those thirteen days:

On Tuesday morning, October 16, President Kennedy revealed to his brother Robert that an American U-2 observation plane had taken startling photos of Cuba from very high altitudes. The photos clearly showed that the Soviets were placing missiles, some of them with nuclear warheads, in Cuba. The missiles were surface-to-surface — and they were set to be launched against the United States.

Robert Kennedy had recently spoken to the Soviet Ambassador to the United States, Anatoly Dobrynin. He had assured Bob that Cuba had no offensive missiles — that was the promise from Soviet Premier Nikita Khrushchev himself, he said. Dobrynin might have been misled. Khrushchev was certainly lying.

Later that morning the Executive Committee ("Ex Comm") of the National Security Council — the top government group concerned with America's safety — met. They were shocked by the missile news. They knew some action had to be taken.

President Kennedy told Ex Comm to come forward with a plan. They were to meet without him — and argue freely. Bob would be their informal chairman and report to him.

Ex Comm's first idea was a blockade, or quarantine. This would be a circle of U.S. warships around Cuba to prevent Soviet cargo vessels from making further missile deliveries.

Some Ex Comm members objected. What about the missiles already on Cuba? Further, they argued, if the United States blockaded Cuba, the Russians would blockade West Berlin, the free city located inside Communist East Germany.

What they wanted was a "surgical" air strike against Cuba. The "surgery" would destroy missiles and launching sites, but — the strike advocates hoped — would avoid hitting Cuban cities and towns. Robert Kennedy favored the blockade. He knew that, no matter how expert the surgery, many thousands of Cubans would be killed.

A day or so later, more U-2 photos showed new sites being set up. With Florida only ninety miles from Cuba, the missile targets would be the major cities of eastern United States and their tens of millions of people.

As Ex Comm continued to argue, Soviet Foreign Minister Andrei Gromyko came to see the president. The meeting had been arranged some time before, and John Kennedy did not wish to cancel it. To do so might show that the United States knew about the missiles. The president wanted to keep that secret for the time being.

Gromyko told the president that the United States should stop threatening Cuba. Cuba wanted only peace, he said, and had no intention of spreading its communism to other Latin American lands. What about the arms Soviet Russia had been shipping to Cuba for years, the president asked. These were for defense, Gromyko replied; they did not endanger the United States. After a time he left. Neither he nor Kennedy had mentioned the nuclear missiles pointed at the United States.

The blockade backers continued to strengthen their argument. The air strike advocates could not overcome one flaw in their plan. No air strike could be "surgically" thorough. It could not guarantee to wipe out *all* the missiles. And even one left intact could be launched and bring untold damage and death in the United States.

By Saturday, October 20, the president had decided on the blockade. America's allies around the world were asked for support. President De Gaulle of France, Chancellor Adenauer of West Germany, Prime Minister Macmillan of Britain all promised to give it. The Organization of American States (OAS) — to which the countries of North and South America belong — voted to stand behind the United States. The OAS vote made the blockade legal in international law.

Congressional leaders were told of the plan. Some liked it. Some wanted stronger action. The president argued that if he took such action right away, millions of American lives would be in danger. There was always time later for air strikes and invasions. On Monday night, October 22, he went on national TV and told the whole story to the American people.

The U.S. Navy sent 180 warships to the Caribbean to set up the blockade. U.S. troops and planes stood by along the East Coast in case the blockade failed and stronger action was required. The nation waited tensely.

Kennedy cabled Khrushchev, telling him that a U.S. blockade around Cuba would prevent Soviet vessels from delivering more missiles. He emphasized that the U.S. Navy did not wish to fire on the Soviet ships. At the end of the cable Kennedy said: "I am concerned that we both show prudence and do nothing to allow events to make the situation more difficult to control than it is." In other words, we must both be very, very careful.

Over and over Kennedy warned his own aides and staff to be careful. A misstep could trigger World War III and wipe out much of mankind. Bob Kennedy went to see Ambassador Dobrynin again. Again Dobrynin denied the existence of offensive missiles on Cuba.

The blockade began Wednesday, October 24. That morning Bob Kennedy told his brother, "If you hadn't acted, you would have been impeached." John Kennedy replied, "That's what I think — I would have been impeached."

On that same morning about twenty Soviet tankers and cargo vessels sailed close to the blockade line. Would they try to cross the line? Would

U.S. warships be forced to stop them?

At the critical moment most of the Soviet vessels turned back. Only the tankers continued on. These were not stopped, because it was unlikely that they carried missiles.

The crisis was still on. U-2 photos on Thursday, October 25, revealed that missile site construction was proceeding even faster. Yet the Americans allowed a Soviet passenger ship, with 1,500 people aboard, to cross the blockade line. Kennedy did not want to stop the ship and risk a fight at that point.

Finally, on Friday, October 26, the U.S. Navy stopped and boarded the cargo vessel *Marucla*. Choosing the *Marucla* as the first ship to be stopped was intentional. It was owned by a Panamanian company, registered in Lebanon, and only leased to the Soviets. Kennedy was showing Khruschev that he intended to enforce the blockade. But, because the *Marucla* was not actually Soviet-owned, the enforcement was less severe. Kennedy was starting slow and playing it cool. The *Marucla* had no missiles aboard and was allowed to go on.

That night Kennedy got a cable from Khruschev. The Soviet boss had undoubtedly written it himself. The cable was long, emotional, wailing about the horror of nuclear war, yet vowing that the Cuban missiles were only for defense.

Eventually Khruschev came to the point: The United States was to withdraw the blockade and promise never to invade Cuba. In turn the Soviet Union would stop shipping missiles to Cuba and take back or destroy any left on the island.

Ex Comm read the cable forward and back, up and down. Before the offer could be acted on, another cable followed. This too was signed by Khrushchev, but it was stiff and formal — obviously written by the Soviet's own Ex Comm. It demanded that the United States lift its missiles from Turkey before the Soviet Union would remove its missiles from Cuba.

It was true that the United States had placed missiles on the Turkish border years ago. These were now old and obsolete. Yet the United States was unwilling to submit to the Soviet demand — to trade Cuban for Turkish missiles. This was not the time to bargain.

Besides, which cable — and which deal — was the United States supposed to accept? The first or the second?

At that point news flashed in that an American U-2 pilot had been shot down over Cuba. Did this mean that the United States must attack and invade Cuba? Did this mean war with Soviet Russia? Did this mean worldwide nuclear destruction?

The Joint Chiefs of Staff argued for an attack. President Kennedy was all for cooling it. He would not be pushed into starting World War III. The President's good sense won out. The United States accepted the U-2 pilot's death without striking back. At Kennedy's direction, a cable was sent to

Khrushchev taking the offer in his first message. The second message was simply ignored.

On Sunday morning, October 28, Khrushchev wired that he would withdraw the missiles. He was sure that everything would work out satisfactorily. And he ended his reply by sending his best wishes to both John and Robert Kennedy. Shrewd Khrushchev was recognizing the second most important man in the U.S. government as well as the first.

The crisis was over — for the moment. But was Cuba already preparing to revenge itself on the United States in another way?

Death in Dallas

President Kennedy continued to face new world problems. At home he had his quarrels with Congress and the Republican party. Nor was it all smooth sailing with his own Democrats. In November, 1963, he saw that he would have to fly to Texas and settle a feud among the bickering factions of the state's Democratic party.

The conservative wing of the Texas party was headed by Governor John Connally (who later switched over to the Republicans). The liberal Texas Democrats were led by Senator Ralph Yarborough. But Vice President Lyndon Johnson, chosen for his post partly for his popularity in Texas, seemed to have lost his following. It was Kennedy's job to keep Texas Democrats happy —

and to make sure they would vote for him in the 1964 election, now a year away.

Yes, Kennedy was already getting ready to run again. He was pretty sure that Senator Barry Goldwater of Arizona was to be his Republican opponent. And he was pretty sure he could beat Goldwater. But Kennedy wasn't taking any chances. He wanted the Texas votes in his pocket.

A president just doesn't drop in on a city or state. His trip requires plans for motorcades, speeches, dedications, dinners, and other showy events. He must have speeches written for him and briefings on all the local leaders who will shake his hand. All this takes time.

Finally, Kennedy was set to fly to Texas. Jacqueline was to go with him. This would be her first public appearance since the previous August, when the Kennedys had lost their newborn son Patrick, who lived only forty hours after birth.

The Kennedy party was to travel in the presidential jet, Air Force One. Vice President Johnson and his wife Lady Bird were to follow in another plane. (Presidents and vice presidents never fly in the same aircraft.)

The evening before they left, the Kennedys held a White House reception for the Supreme Court and other members of the judicial branch. Later that evening Robert Kennedy celebrated his thirty-eighth birthday. He and Ethel entertained sixty guests at Hickory Hill, their home in McLean, Virginia. Bob sat up until two A.M., talking to actor-dancer Gene Kelly.

First presidential stop: San Antonio, Texas, on Thursday, November 21.

San Antonians at the airport enthusiastically welcomed the Kennedys. Everyone cheered and clamored for Jackie. She was the one they had come to see. They clapped and shouted when she gave a short speech — in Spanish — to a group of Latin American voters. The president later spoke at a political dinner for Congressman Albert Thomas, a faithful Texas Democrat.

That same evening, back in Washington, D.C., Senator Hubert Humphrey made a strangely prophetic remark. Speaking to the National Association for Mental Health, he warned that "the act of an emotionally disturbed person or irresponsible citizen can strike down a great leader." It may only have been coincidence. Or Humphrey may have been unknowingly making a grim forecast of the next day's murder.

And was it only idle talk when Kennedy himself told his wife the next morning, "You know, last night would have been . . . a night to assassinate a President?" Continuing, he said, "I mean it. There was the rain and the night, and we were all getting jostled. Suppose a man had a pistol and a briefcase." He gestured with thumb and forefinger, as if firing a gun. "Then he could have dropped the gun and briefcase — and melted into the crowd."

58

The schedule was hectic. Right after the Thomas speech, the Kennedys and their party flew to Fort Worth, arriving after midnight. Next morning — the morning of the fatal day, November 22, 1963 — John Kennedy was up and about early. The crowds gathered around the hotel kept asking for Jackie. He quieted them by saying, "Mrs. Kennedy is organizing herself. It takes her a little longer, but of course she looks better than we do when she does it."

Jacqueline appeared eventually, wearing a pink suit trimmed in blue and a blue pillbox hat. This was the outfit she wore, soon bloodstained and crushed, through that awful day. She refused to discard it until late that night, after the body of her husband had been properly cared for. It is an outfit the world remembers her in, in the thousands of feet of film and the countless news photos shot on that Black Friday.

After Kennedy spoke to the Fort Worth Chamber of Commerce, their motorcade left for the airport and the thirteen-minute flight to Dallas. Air Force One set down at Love Field, Dallas, at 11:37 A.M.

Dallas is a rangy, rawboned town, both Southern and Western. Its people are loud in their love for Texas — its size, its frontier history, its championship college football teams. Many Dallasites are members of rich oil and cattle families. The majority of Dallas voters are Democrats, but on the conservative side.

As such, a fair member of Dallas voters didn't

like John F. Kennedy. He was a Northerner and an Easterner, a product of Boston and of Harvard University, a Catholic and a liberal. He stood for a different tradition than the one Dallas was used to.

Kennedy was warned beforehand that he would meet an undercurrent of hostility in Dallas. Governor Connally was against his visit to the city, saying, "Dallas people are too emotional." U.S. Senator J. William Fulbright of Arkansas — he knew Dallas well — told the president, "Dallas is a very dangerous city."

The clearest forecast of trouble had come when Adlai Stevenson visited Dallas less than a month before. Stevenson, U.S. ambassador to the United Nations, was in town on October 24 for United Nations Day. As U.N. ambassador, and as former governor of Illinois and twice the Democratic candidate for president, Stevenson was entitled to courtesy and respect. Yet Dallas mobs cursed him, spat on him, and hit him with a placard. It was a terrifying experience, even for an old politician like Stevenson.

Kennedy knew, of course, about the attack on Stevenson. But he didn't take it or the warnings too seriously. Those were the chances a man in public had to take, he probably told himself.

And he knew that he was not popular everywhere. After all, he had won the presidency by only a narrow margin. Just about half of all the U.S. voters had cast their ballots for somebody else. He knew too that every city had its share of Kennedy-haters. There was no reason to suspect that Dallas was any worse.

The crowd at Love Field was boisterously friendly. Vice President Johnson, Governor Connally, and Senator Yarborough were among the welcomers. Kennedy shook hands and joshed with some of the crowd, then took his place in the presidential limousine. At 11:15 A.M. the motorcade was ready to depart.

In the lead car, an unmarked white Ford, were Secret Service men and county and city police officials. Then came three police motorcyclists. Following the cycles was SS 100X, the president's car (a specially constructed Lincoln convertible, with the top down). Secret Service Agent Bill Greer was driving. Next to him sat Agent Roy Kellerman. The rear section had two jump seats, occupied by Governor Connally and his wife, Nellie. In the back sat John and Jacqueline Kennedy.

The follow-up car came next, with presidential aides Ken O'Donnell and Dave Powers as passengers, and seven Secret Service men — including Clint Hill — ready to protect the president and his wife. On the back seat lay a powerful AR-15 .223 automatic rifle.

Next in the motorcade line was the vice president's car carrying Lyndon and Lady Bird Johnson and Senator and Mrs. Ralph Yarborough, with Agent Rufus Youngblood in the front seat. Behind it was another police car. The press pool car, equipped with a radiophone, followed. Then came the press photographers' car. The remainder of the motorcade trailed behind.

The motorcade's destination was the Dallas Trade Mart. There Kennedy was to speak at a luncheon. And there the unity of the Texas Democrats, liberal and conservative, was to be on display.

On the way the president saw a group of little children holding up a sign: MR. PRESIDENT: PLEASE STOP AND SHAKE OUR HANDS. He halted the procession and got out of SS 100X. The children gathered around him and clutched at his hands with great glee.

Most of the cheering along the route seemed to be for Mrs. Kennedy. "Jackiiieee!" the crowds shouted. Her husband was pleased.

The motorcade reached Main Street and turned west to travel along it for twelve downtown blocks. At Dealey Plaza the route plan called for a turn north on Houston Street, then, after a block, a sharp turn west on Elm Street. Elm Street was to take the procession through an underpass to a ramp leading up and out to Stemmons Freeway. From there the Trade Mart was only five minutes away.

At the northwest corner of Houston and Elm Streets stood the Texas School Book Depository. This was a warehouse maintained by a group of textbook publishers to fill orders for textbooks from local schools. It was the noon hour, and most of the warehouse workers were outside watching the motorcade go by.

At 12:30 P.M. the motorcade had made its turn west from Houston to Elm and was proceeding at a speed of about eleven miles an hour. The crowd kept on cheering. One man, Abraham Zapruder, had his 8-mm color movie camera focused on the president's car.

The scene seemed so friendly, so normal, so American. Then, in an instant, everything changed.

A Nation Mourns

Suddenly, rifle shots, three at least, banged out. The President was hit, surely fatally. Blood, bone, and tissue spattered from his head — over Mrs. Kennedy, over Governor Connally in the seat ahead. John Kennedy crumpled. Jacqueline held him close to her, as if to protect him from further harm.

Governor Connally had been hit, too. He collapsed moaning against Nellie Connally. The Secret Service agents and the police were confused, numb with shock and horror. They had never seen anything like this before.

Then Agent Clint Hill leaped from the car behind and threw himself on the trunk of SS 100X. With Jackie's help he wriggled forward and hovered over the presidential pair. Seeing Kennedy's fatal wounds, Hill beat against the trunk with his fist.

The shooting spanned about twenty-two seconds. During that time Zapruder took more than four hundred frames of color film. They became an invaluable record of the tragedy.

During those same seconds Agent Kellerman, seated to the right of the SS 100X driver, grabbed his microphone and shouted to the lead car, "We are hit! Get us to a hospital!" With that, most of the motorcade sped forward, up the ramp to Stemmons Freeway, then north to Harry Hines Boulevard, and on to Parkland Memorial Hospital. The four-mile trip took six minutes.

On the way, the press pool reporters radiophoned the first news of the tragedy to their media. Within minutes, after the shooting, America and the world knew that something terrible had happened.

SS 100X stopped at the Parkland emergency entrance. Jacqueline still held her husband close to her. Clint Hill told her that Kennedy would have to be taken inside. She answered, "You know he's dead, Mr. Hill. Let me alone."

Eventually she let go of the president and allowed him to be placed on a stretcher. Governor Connally was conscious, but in great pain. He was bleeding from wounds in the chest and wrist. Lifted from the car, he was carried by stretcher into the hospital along with the president.

Later, a spent bullet was found by the side of the two stretchers. Its tip was in nearly perfect condition. Apparently it encountered little resistance in hitting Kennedy or Connally — or both. This bullet's condition, as we shall see, has never been satisfactorily explained.

John Kennedy was carried into Trauma Room 1. The doctor on emergency duty saw at once that there was no hope. Nevertheless, he went ahead with his lifesaving measures. Two gunshot wounds could be seen: a great hole in the right rear of the head, oozing blood and brain tissue, and a hole in the throat just above the Adam's apple. The president's heart still beat faintly, and his pulse could be counted.

The doctor enlarged the throat wound to let in air for breathing. A blood transfusion program was started. The president's chest was pumped to keep his heart beating. Other emergency steps were taken.

But it was no use. President John F. Kennedy died on the operating table.

The time was exactly 1:00 P.M.

The news was flashed around the world: JOHN F. KENNEDY ASSASSINATED! The world held its breath awaiting further news. Was it a plot to destroy the U.S. government? Which leader, American or foreign, would be next?

Lyndon Johnson might have been next in the line of the assassin's fire. As soon as the first shot was heard, however, Agent Youngblood shielded the vice president with his own body. His car was in the motorcade that sped to Parkland Hospital. On arrival, the Johnsons were hustled into an empty room under Secret Service guard. Soon they got word that Kennedy had died.

Experts on the U.S. Constitution say that when a president dies, his vice president automatically becomes president. Taking the presidential oath of office is only a ceremony, they say. But Lyndon Johnson was not sure of this. He phoned the attorney general, Robert Kennedy, in Washington to make sure of the proper steps.

Home at Hickory Hill for lunch, Bob Kennedy had already heard the news. FBI Director J. Edgar Hoover had told him over the phone. Bob was stunned too deeply for tears. Another Kennedy struck down! Of the nine children, two sons and a daughter gone — who would be next?

Bob advised Lyndon Johnson, still at Parkland Hospital, to take the oath of office as soon as possible, just to be sure. He also advised the new president to return to Washington at once. The world must know that the United States is never leaderless — that men may die, but stable and orderly government goes on.

At the same time the Kennedy aides, headed by Ken O'Donnell and Larry O'Brien, were struggling to leave Dallas immediately with their dead chief. In their grief and rage they seemed to hold all Dallas responsible for the tragedy. They wanted nothing more to do with the city. So they called for a coffin to be delivered to Parkland Hospital. Filled with its sad burden, the coffin was pushed and shoved out of the hospital, back to Love Field, and onto Air Force One. Several local officials tried to stop the Kennedy men, but they would not be stopped.

What they were doing was probably illegal. At that time, the murder of a president was a crime against state law only — after Kennedy's death, it became a crime against federal law. With the body gone it was impossible for the state-appointed coroner to conduct an autopsy and inquest, as required by state law. And without such steps, there might not be legal proof that a murder had taken place. The accused slayer, if he were caught, might have to be set free.

This did not matter to the Kennedy party. Only one thing was on their minds — get out of Dallas and get back to Washington. Mrs. Kennedy agreed.

As for Lyndon Johnson, he, too, was in a hurry. So a federal judge was found to administer the presidential oath of office to Johnson in the crowded main stateroom of Air Force One. Lady Bird stood beside him as he was sworn in. So did Jacqueline Kennedy, still in her blood-spattered pink suit. Through the whole ordeal she never gave way. She held tight to her dignity and control.

The judge read the simple oath, and Johnson repeated it phrase by phrase: "I do solemnly swear that I will faithfully execute the Office of President of the United States, and will to the best of my ability preserve, protect, and defend the Constitution of the United States." The judge added, "So help me God," and Lyndon Johnson repeated those words, too. The new president had officially taken office.

At 2:47 P.M., Central Standard Time, Air Force One took to the sky. John Kennedy had been dead only an hour and forty-seven minutes.

It was about 6:00 P.M., Eastern Standard Time, already dusk, when Air Force One hit the runway at Andrews Air Force Base just outside Washington. First to board the plane on its arrival was Robert Kennedy. He greeted Jacqueline quietly.

A fork-lift truck hoisted the coffin off the plane and into a waiting ambulance. The ambulance was headed for Bethesda Naval Hospital. There a post-mortem (after-death) examination was to be performed. Bob, Jackie, and an Air Force officer rode in the ambulance, sitting on the floor next to the coffin.

Kennedy's body was X-rayed, the wounds photographed, and the vital organs examined to learn the exact cause of death. Then it was embalmed and placed in a mahogany coffin (the Dallas-procured coffin had been damaged in the rush to leave the city). The new coffin, with the Kennedy party following, was borne to the White House long after midnight.

Lyndon Johnson had gone directly by helicopter from Andrews Air Force Base to the White House. The president's Oval Office had already been cleared of John Kennedy's personal things. Johnson sat at the stripped-down desk and made some important phone calls. He told the assembled staff,

"There must be no gap. The government must go forward — we've had a tremendous shock, and we have to keep going."

Then he wrote, by hand, a letter to each of the Kennedy children. To Caroline he wrote: "Your father's death has been a great tragedy for the Nation, as well as for you, and I wanted you to know how much my thoughts are of you at this time. He was a wise and devoted man. You can always be proud of what he did for his country . . ."

To John he said: "It will be many years before you understand fully what a great man your father was. His loss is a deep personal tragedy for all of us, but I wanted you particularly to know that I share your grief. . . . You can always be proud of him. . . ."

Lyndon Johnson was devoted to his own two daughters. For the rest of his life he also watched over Caroline and John Kennedy, Jr.

Back at Dallas's Parkland Hospital, Governor Connally was sleeping soundly, out of danger. The assassin's bullet had smashed a rib and the left wrist, and collapsed a lung in tearing through Connally's body. The operation was successful, and in time he would come out well and whole. Now, as he slept, Texas Rangers guarded his room.

In the White House solemn and stately funeral arrangements were being made. The coffin was placed in the East Room on a black catafalque, like the one used for the slain president Lincoln nearly a century before. The Death Watch — a military honor guard, changed every half hour — was posted. Included were soldiers of the Special Forces wearing their green berets. John Kennedy had been relying on these skilled fighters to help settle the mounting crisis in Vietnam.

The chandeliers were draped in black. Candles flickered, and priests knelt in prayer around the coffin. And all that day, and on the following days, TV brought people close to the showy ceremonies and the genuine grief that take place when a well-loved American president is assassinated.

TV watchers around the world grieved along with the mourners who attended the rites. Radio Moscow played nothing but funeral music. Britain's Queen Elizabeth ordered her court into mourning for a week. In Paris, Americans far from home wept openly. In Dunganstown, Ireland, birthplace of the Patrick Kennedy who came to the United States, shops were closed and curtains drawn.

In Shiokawa, Japan, Mayor Kohei Hanami said, "The world has lost an irreplaceable man." Twenty years before, Hanami had been the captain of the destroyer *Amagiri* which rammed and sank *PT-109*. Sixty thousand West Berliners gathered at City Hall Square in the rain to show their sorrow.

It was raining in Washington, too. Across the street from the White House, a silent crowd stood vigil under the dripping trees in Lafayette Square.

They watched while black limousines discharged their passengers, American and foreign dignitaries, under the North Portico. The sad day dragged on.

On Sunday morning, November 24, the sun shone brightly on the city. About noon a procession formed to escort the coffin to the Capitol. Six matched gray horses pulled a black-draped caisson (ammunition wagon) up the White House driveway. The coffin was gently placed on the caisson, and the cortège started up Pennsylvania Avenue.

In the cortège were soldiers, sailors, and marines marching to the muffled tattoo of drums. Behind the caisson an army man led Black Jack, a riderless black horse. A silver sword hung from Black Jack's saddle. Cavalry boots and spurs were reversed in the stirrups. Empty reversed boots are an ancient symbol of a warrior slain in battle.

Jacqueline Kennedy, her two children, and the new president and his wife rode in a black limousine. Cars bearing other notables followed. The Joint Chiefs of Staff marched with their troops.

At the Capitol the coffin was carried up the steps to the Rotunda while the U.S. Navy Band played slowly. There the body lay in state, as tributes were paid to John F. Kennedy. The public formed a line twenty blocks long to file past the bier for a last good-bye.

On Monday morning, November 25, the coffin

was first taken back to the White House, then to St. Matthew's Cathedral, where a pontifical requiem mass, one of the most solemn rites of the Roman Catholic Church, was to be held.

The Kennedy party and a great crowd of mourners walked behind the caisson to the cathedral. Walking with the Kennedys were such world leaders as French President Charles de Gaulle, Britain's Prince Philip, and Emperor Haile Selassie of Ethiopia, all in military dress. Washington police and the FBI were out in full force to protect this distinguished assemblage.

Cardinal Richard Cushing of Boston, close friend of the Kennedy family, conducted the Mass. He had married John and Jacqueline Kennedy; he had buried their infant son Patrick. Now he performed the saddest task of his priestly career. TV viewers of every faith were deeply moved as they watched.

The cardinal closed the largely Latin Mass by adding, in English, a prayer of his own: "May the angels, dear Jack, lead you into Paradise. May the martyrs receive you at your coming. May the spirit of God embrace you, and mayest thou, with all those who made the supreme sacrifice of dying for others, receive eternal rest and peace. Amen."

The Mass completed and the band playing "Hail to the Chief," the cortège moved on to Arlington National Cemetery. It was raining again. Amid great pomp and ceremony — and very real sadness and sorrow — the body of John F. Kennedy was lowered into the ground. Jacqueline lighted the Eternal Flame, and the funeral was over.

By all rights, John Kennedy should have then taken his place in the past. But the past does not accept its dead until disturbing questions are settled. The dead remain upon the consciences of the living as long as doubts exist.

The major question, the deep doubt, burning today in the minds of many Americans is: Who was really responsible for the murder of John F. Kennedy?

Oswald—
Was He the Only One?

The search to identify John Kennedy's killer — or killers — and the reasons for his (or their) act can begin at the time and place where it all happened: 12:30 P.M., November 22, 1963, at Dallas, Texas.

At that moment, three employees of the Texas School Book Depository were at the building's fifth-floor windows watching the motorcade pass. One of them saw President Kennedy raise his right arm as if to wave to the crowd. Then the man heard what sounded like a rifle shot. Startled, he said to the others, "I believe someone is shooting at the president!"

Another noise, this time from overhead, was heard. This sounded like a shell casing had dropped on the floor above. Still another shot resounded, and a shower of plaster fell from the ceiling onto the three men. Two of them put their heads outside the windows, looking up.

A news photographer in the motorcade below saw them do so. He, too, looked up at the window of the floor above, the sixth floor. "Look up in the window!" he yelled to the other cameramen in the car. "There's the rifle!"

In the motorcade's lead car Dallas Police Chief Jesse Curry heard the shots. Through his car's two-way radio he ordered a cop to investigate the top of the underpass. In the third auto, the Secret Service Car, Agent Forrest Sorrels believed the shots were coming from the grassy knoll beyond the underpass. Many people on the underpass top and on the knoll thought the shots were coming from behind them.

Motorcycle Officer Marrion Baker noted pigeons scattering from the roof and eaves of the Book Depository. He wheeled his cycle around and sped toward the building. Rushing in, he found building manager Roy Truly. Together they began a quick search of the floors.

It was only 12:32 when they found a slight young man on the second floor landing. Wearing a white shirt, he calmly leaned against a vending machine and drank a Coca-Cola. Baker thrust his gun into the young man's midsection and demanded of Truly, "Do you know this man? Does he work here?" Truly answered, "Yes," and the two hurried along on their search.

The young man was Lee Harvey Oswald, age twenty-four. The elements demand close analysis, for they are puzzling and contradictory. They neither establish his complete innocence nor his sole responsibility for the assassination. They seem to say, rather, that Oswald was part of a plan, a member of a conspiracy.

The very incomplete evidence also suggests that Oswald was meant to be caught and to take the blame. Oswald seemed to realize this, too. Hours before his death two days after he was arrested, he said, "I was a patsy."

Finishing his Coke, Oswald walked outside and caught a bus. The bus, however, became tied up in the traffic turmoil at Dealey Plaza. He left the bus and flagged down a cab at the nearby Greyhound Bus terminal. An old lady was also waiting for a taxi. Oswald, apparently in no hurry, offered his cab to her. She declined, so Oswald climbed in, and the taxi drove off.

At his rooming house, Oswald — observed by the housekeeper — went into his room. He came out wearing a dark jacket with a zipper closure. In his waistband, it was discovered later, was a .38-caliber revolver. He paused at the front door for a few minutes, as if waiting for someone. Then he walked toward the Texas Theater, a movie house several blocks away.

The alarm was already out for Oswald. The Dallas Police, the Secret Service, and the FBI had decided he had fired the shots from the School Book Depository that killed John Kennedy and wounded Governor Connally.

An officer in a police cruiser heard the alarm and was on the lookout for Oswald in the area. He was J. D. Tippit, an eleven-year veteran of the Dallas police force. For a reason that has never been explained, he pulled over to the curb and got out of the car. Someone fired a gun at him several times. Officer Tippit fell dead, four bullets in his head.

Who was Tippit's murderer? Witnesses on the scene gave confused and contradictory descriptions. He was a tall man, a short man, with straight or wavy hair, wearing a dark or light jacket. He was alone; he was with a companion.

Within seconds of the shooting, police cars zeroed in. Soon they got the word: A suspect had been seen hurrying into the Texas Theater.

About two dozen people were in the darkened theater watching a movie called *War Is Hell*. The police swarmed in, turned on the house lights, and began their search. Officer N. M. McDonald later said that an unidentified man in the front row had tipped him off — the person they were looking for was sitting in the back of the theater. McDonald headed for that person. He was Lee Harvey Oswald.

As McDonald closed in, Oswald said, "It's all over now." McDonald reached for him. Oswald hit the officer in the face, grabbing for his own revolver at the same time. The two fought for possession of the gun.

By this time other policemen were throwing themselves on the struggling Oswald. They pinned his arms and held him still. As they dragged him from the theater, he kept shouting, "I am not resisting arrest! I protest this police brutality!"

The police were sure they had caught Tippit's murderer. They were also sure the same man had murdered John Kennedy.

Oswald was swiftly taken to the Dallas Police and Courts Building. For the rest of that day and until deep in the night, he was fingerprinted, searched, questioned, and shown in police lineups for identification by witnesses.

Before being questioned, Oswald was advised of his legal rights. He would not be forced to say anything. Anything he did say, however, could be used against him. And he was entitled to choose his own lawyer.

Oswald later tried to call a left-wing lawyer, John Abt, in New York, but could not reach him. He then said he would be satisfied with any lawyer supplied by the Dallas chapter of the American Civil Liberties Union. This organization later said that it had never received Oswald's request for counsel. So Oswald never had an attorney.

At midnight a short press conference was held. It was taped for later showings. Oswald protested to the reporters about the lengthy police questioning and the lineups. He felt that his rights were being violated. Another violation of standard police procedure was also going on. The question sessions were not taped, nor was a stenographer on hand to take them down in shorthand. Thus no record exists of what the police asked Oswald or what he replied.

Oswald denied any guilt in the murders of Kennedy and Tippit. He was calm in his denials. In *The Assassination Tapes* (1975), author George O'Toole claimed that the press conference tapes show Oswald was telling the truth. O'Toole, a former CIA man, based his claim on electronic analysis of Oswald's voice. The method, said O'Toole, works something like a lie detector. It shows up stress in the person speaking.

Next day the questioning began again. Oswald was allowed to see his mother and brother briefly. But he was unable to reach his wife, Marina. Even today a cloud of doubt hangs over the relationship between Oswald and Marina.

The police were sure that they had tracked down the killer. Captain Will Fritz of Homicide said, "I think the case is cinched." District Attorney Henry Wade said, "I have no doubts in this case. There is no question Oswald was the killer of President Kennedy."

In making these statements, the authorities were going beyond their legal limits. However guilty Oswald seemed, they had no right to say such things. "Innocent until *proven* guilty" should have been their maxim.

On Sunday morning Oswald was questioned further for about two hours. Then preparations were made to transfer him to the County Jail. This was about thirteen blocks away from the Courts Building where he had been held since Friday afternoon. A decoy armored truck was brought into the basement of the Courts Building. Oswald was actually to travel in an unmarked police cruiser by a different route.

The public was supposed to be barred from the basement, but reporters and photographers were admitted freely. There were at least seventy policemen in the basement to prevent any sort of trouble.

Handcuffed, Oswald was brought down by elevator to the basement at 11:20 A.M. An officer had hold of each arm, but there was no one in front of Oswald. TV cameras were bringing the live scene to audiences all over the country.

Suddenly — just as suddenly as John Kennedy had been slain — a man stepped forward in full view of the TV cameras. He fired one shot from a .38-caliber revolver at Lee Harvey Oswald. Oswald fell, fatally wounded.

At once the police grappled with the killer and took his gun. He was a man well-known to both police and press — a Dallas nightclub owner named Jack Ruby, age fifty-two. Ruby was locked up, to be questioned later.

Oswald was rushed to the same Parkland Memorial Hospital where John Kennedy had died and where Governor Connally was slowly recovering. The one bullet had done its work. Oswald died on the operating table at 12:40 P.M.

With the murder of Oswald added to the slayings of John Kennedy and Officer Tippit, the search for reasons and motives quickened. The Dallas police, the Texas Rangers (Texas' state troopers), and the FBI went all out in their search for evidence.

President Johnson, however, wanted a special group to investigate the triple killings. A week after that fatal Friday, he appointed The President's Commission on the Assassination of President Kennedy. Johnson asked Chief Justice Earl Warren to head the commission. At first Warren refused.

The new president soon persuaded Warren to take the assignment. He said that only a man who ranked as high as the Chief Justice could settle rumors from abroad that the nation itself was in danger. Johnson wanted the world to know that the United States remained strong and stable. He also wanted the investigation settled before the next presidential election, now less then a year away.

Other members of the Warren Commission were U.S. Senator Richard B. Russell, Democrat of Georgia; U.S. Senator John Sherman Cooper, Republican of Kentucky; U.S. Representative Hale Boggs, Democrat of Louisiana; U.S. Representative Gerald R. Ford, Republican of Michigan; Allen Dulles, former director of the CIA; and John J.

McCloy, who had held several important government posts. Gerald Ford, at forty-nine, was the youngest member of the commission.

All the members were busy men. None could give full time to the investigation. A staff of fifteen lawyers, headed by J. Lee Rankin, former solicitor general of the United States, actually directed the task. The staff was assisted by many field investigators.

Beginning in February, 1964, the staff heard the stories of 552 witnesses. The staff also gathered files full of documents and photos relating to the crimes. On September 24, 1964 — ten months after the slayings — the commission presented its one-volume Warren Report to the president. Following the report came twenty-six volumes of the hearings — fifteen volumes of witnesses' testimony and eleven of exhibits.

The general conclusion of the Warren Report: Lee Harvey Oswald — and Oswald alone — killed President Kennedy and Officer Tippit, and wounded Governor Connally.

Was the conclusion of the Warren Report correct?

Enter Marguerite and Marina

The Warren Report gives a detailed story of the crimes. But it omits or skips over some important facts, and makes mistakes about some others.

Did these flaws creep in because the report had to be produced in such a hurry?

Or were they made intentionally — to hide certain truths that might endanger the nation's security? Some of the data was locked up for seventy-five years. When unlocked, will this data tell anything new? Will it matter by then?

In discussing the Oswald family, the report tells a good deal about Lee Harvey Oswald's mother. The report tends to picture her as somewhat ignorant, stubborn, and out for herself. For years after the murders, Mrs. Oswald claimed that her son was innocent. Perhaps it was only mother love, family pride, stubbornness. Yet Mrs. Oswald may have had hold of something the investigators failed to see.

Marguerite Claverie Oswald was born in 1907 in New Orleans. She was first married to John Pic, father of their son, John, Jr. Divorcing Pic, she married Robert E. Oswald. They had two sons, Robert, Jr., and Lee Harvey. Lee never saw his father; he died two months before Lee was born in 1939. Later, Marguerite married Edwin A. Eckdahl. They were divorced in a few years, and Marguerite chose thereafter to call herself Mrs. Oswald.

Marguerite had to work between marriages and after her last one. The three boys were sometimes in orphan homes or boarding schools, sometimes looked after by neighbors after school. The fatherless family settled in Fort Worth, Texas. There the two older boys grew up in a normal way. Lee early began to display disturbing signs.

In grade school he was a poor pupil. He never learned to spell, and even as an adult his spelling was atrocious. He read widely, but scored low on reading tests. Making few friends, he preferred to be alone. When he was with others, he often showed a violent temper.

After high school, John, Jr., joined the Coast Guard, and Robert, the Marines. In 1952, Mrs. Oswald and Lee moved to New York City to be with John, who was stationed there. She found a job, and Lee, now thirteen, was enrolled in public school. But as soon as Mrs. Oswald left for work each morning, Lee returned to their apartment to stay by himself all day. Once he quarreled with John's wife and threatened her with a knife.

Because of his generally bad behavior, the boy was taken into custody. Juvenile authorities had Lee examined by a psychiatrist. He was found to have "definite traits of dangerousness." At Youth House, a social agency, Lee was said to be "seriously withdrawn, detached, and emotionally isolated." But Marguerite Oswald's response to probation officers was, "Please keep out of family affairs."

After about a year in New York, mother and son moved back to New Orleans. For several terms Lee attended school regularly, making low but passing grades. Early in the tenth grade, however, he quit school. Restless and rootless, Marguerite and Lee returned to Fort Worth. Lee started school again. He didn't stay long.

Dropping out, Lee talked of little but wanting to join the Marine Corps. His brother Robert had by then been a Marine for three years, and Lee at sixteen tried to enlist. He was turned down, but he kept on studying the Marine Corps manual. "He knew it by heart," said his mother.

At the same time he began to read Communist books and pamphlets. Most teenagers find Communist literature dull and boring, but Oswald managed to get something out of what he read. Thereafter Oswald took an active interest in communism. However — and this is one of the puzzling things about him — from time to time he claimed to be strongly anti-Communist.

Right after his seventeenth birthday, Lee enlisted in the Marine Corps. He was a Marine for nearly three years, never rising above private first class. The Warren Report spends little time on Oswald's Marine service. It does state that in rifle practice he qualified as a sharpshooter, the middle rank between marksman (low) and expert (high).

The report also tells that Oswald was a loner, that his nickname was Ozzie Rabbit, and that he argued with everybody. According to the report, Oswald was trained as a radar operator and assigned to the 1st Marine Aircraft Wing at Atsugi, Japan. His job was "to direct aircraft to their targets by radar, communicating with the pilot by radio. The squadron also had the duty of scouting for incoming foreign aircraft, such as stray Russian or Chinese planes, which would be intercepted by American planes."

What the Warren Report doesn't mention is that Atsugi was one of the biggest CIA installations around the globe. It sent out high-flying U-2 observation planes over China. It monitored Chinese radio communications. From Atsugi, U.S. planes carried Nationalist Chinese spies who parachuted onto the China mainland.

Only the most trusted radar operators could work at Atsugi. Oswald must have been thoroughly checked out before he got the assignment. It didn't seem to matter that he had been court-martialed twice, once for shooting himself, accidentally, with his own .22-caliber pistol (possessing such a weapon was prohibited), the second, for swearing at a non-commissioned officer and pouring a drink over him.

And no one asked questions when Oswald began studying the Russian language on his own at Atsugi. By the time he was transferred to El Toro Air Station in California, he spoke and read Russian well. (He was never tested on his Russian spelling, however.) Other marines sometimes called him "Oswaldskovich." He called them "comrade."

In September, 1959, three months before his hitch was up, Oswald got a "dependency discharge." His mother, he explained, had been hurt and could no longer work. It was true that Marguerite had been injured. But that was a year before, and she was away from her job only a week. Nevertheless, Oswald got his discharge in a few days. Usually it takes several weeks to handle all the paper work in such a discharge.

Now the puzzle becomes more complicated. Oswald was home in Fort Worth only three days. Then — as if acting under orders — he took off. His destination: the Soviet Union.

At New Orleans he boarded a cargo vessel that docked in Le Havre, France. Crossing the Channel to England, he stayed one night. From England he flew to Helsinki, Finland, where he applied for a visa that would let him enter Soviet Russia. He

1.

1. House in Brookline, Mass., suburb of Boston, where John and Robert Kennedy were born.

2. John Kennedy, age 12, was a member of football team of Dexter School, private elementary school in Brookline. (1927)

2.

3.

3. John Kennedy, senior at Harvard College and majoring in government, reads in daily newspaper about Hitler's tactics on Western Front in World War II. (1939)

4. John Kennedy as PT boat commander in World War II. (1943)

5. Robert Kennedy being sworn into Navy as father, Joseph (*left*), looks on. (Oct. 11, 1943)

4.

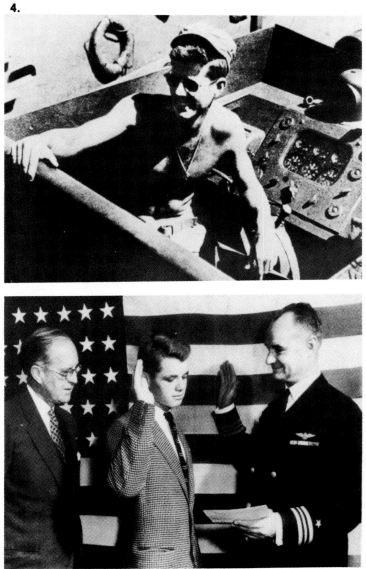

5.

6.

6. Sen. Joseph McCarthy, Republican, of Wisconsin (*center*), confers with Sen. Stuart Symington, Democrat, of Missouri (*left*), member of McCarthy's subcommittee investigating Communists in government, and committee minority counsel Robert Kennedy. (Mar. 10, 1954)

7.

7. Robert Kennedy (*left*), counsel of Senate committee on racketeering in labor and industry, and brother, Senator John Kennedy of Massachusetts, member of committee, confer at hearing about International Brotherhood of Teamsters. (Feb. 27, 1957)

8.

9

8. One of last press pictures of President John Kennedy and his family. They had just finished watching performance by Black Watch. Caroline was almost six, John, Jr., almost two. (Nov. 14, 1963)

9. Body of John Fitzgerald Kennedy lies in repose in historic East Room of White House. Honor guard was made up of one enlisted man from each of four armed services — Army, Navy, Marines, and Air Force. (Nov. 23, 1963)

10.

10. Chief Justice Earl Warren *(left)* hands Pres. Lyndon Johnson, at White House, Warren Commission's voluminous report on John Kennedy's assassination. Warren headed 7-member panel that investigated slaying. Representative Gerald Ford, Republican, of Michigan, was vice-chairman of Warren Commission. (Sept. 24, 1964)

left Helsinki by train and was in Moscow by October 16, 1959.

Why did he leave home so fast? The Warren Report doesn't say. Before he left for Russia his bank balance was $203. His travel expenses must have been at least $1,500. Where did he get the money? The normal waiting time for a visa is one to two weeks. Oswald got his in two days. How so quickly? The Warren Report brushes over these questions.

On Oswald's first day in Moscow, a young woman guide from Intourist (the Soviet government travel bureau) took him sightseeing. He told the guide that he wanted to become a Soviet citizen. She helped him write a letter of application. During the next few days Oswald was interviewed once, perhaps twice. His interviewers were probably from the KGB, the Russian equivalent of the CIA.

On October 25, five days after he arrived in Moscow, Oswald was told his visa had expired and that he must leave the country in two hours. Oswald's answer was to attempt suicide by slashing his wrist. Luckily for Oswald, the Intourist guide turned up just then and rushed him to the hospital.

Oswald was held in the hospital for a week. He still pleaded that he wanted to become a Soviet citizen. Officials told him they would consider his request.

After three more days in his hotel room, Oswald went to the American Embassy. There he told the

Foreign Service Officer that he wanted to renounce his U.S. citizenship. Further, he said, he was ready to turn over to the Soviets the secrets he'd learned as a Marine radar operator. He handed his passport over to the American official to prove that he was serious.

The official told Oswald to return in two days. Instead, Oswald wrote the embassy a letter demanding that it cancel his citizenship. The letter was remarkable, in a way: it had only two misspelled words. Obviously somebody else prepared it, and Oswald copied it out in his own handwriting.

The embassy just let matters stand. Oswald's passport was filed and his record kept open. Other Americans who had previously asked for Soviet citizenship eventually changed their minds. Perhaps the embassy thought that Oswald would, too. Or perhaps the embassy, part of the U.S. State Department, was under orders to act as it did about Oswald.

In January, 1960, a few months after Oswald came to Soviet Russia, he was given permission to stay in the country. However, he was not granted Soviet citizenship. He was classified as a "resident alien" and was issued a "stateless" passport to use for identification.

From Moscow he was sent to the city of Minsk, 450 miles to the southwest. There he was given a job in a factory that made radio and television parts. He was also given a free apartment and a special allowance in addition to his pay.

Oswald seemed to resent his unskilled job. But he apparently liked his income and his living quarters, both good by Soviet standards. He bragged that he lived better than his boss, the factory foreman. At a dance one night about mid-March, 1961, he met a pretty girl, Marina Prusakova.

Marina was nineteen and a graduate pharmacist, a member of Komsomol, the young Communists' organization. She lived in the home of her uncle, a colonel in the MVD, the Soviet secret police. The Warren Report is silent about the influence this uncle may have had on Oswald.

Oswald and Marina were married about a month and a half after they met. Even before this, Oswald had already changed his mind about staying in the Soviet Union. On February 5, 1961, he wrote the American Embassy in Moscow asking that he be allowed to return to the United States.

Under ordinary circumstances, an American who marries a Russian in the Soviet Union has a hard time leaving the country with his or her mate. Oswald must have known this — or maybe he knew something else the Warren Report isn't telling. Even the baby, June Lee, born ten months after the marriage, did not prevent the three from leaving.

They were granted permission to leave in January, 1962, and departed five months later, when June was old enough to travel. The American Embassy lent Oswald $435.71 for travel expenses. The family traveled by train to Holland, passing through the Iron Curtain between East and West Berlin. They had no trouble in crossing this border — and Oswald's passport was not even stamped there. Several critics have wondered why.

At Rotterdam, Holland, the Oswalds boarded a ship bound for Hoboken, New Jersey. Neither the CIA nor the FBI questioned Oswald on arrival. The Warren Report is silent on this fact. Both the CIA and the FBI certainly knew that Oswald had learned radar secrets at Atsugi, Japan, and elsewhere. Both knew that he had threatened to turn these secrets over to Soviet intelligence. The puzzle deepens.

The Oswalds settled in the Dallas-Fort Worth area. Lee drifted from job to job, seemingly unable to find work that interested him and that he could do well. The Oswalds lived simply on the low earnings he brought home. Or was his pay his only source of income?

A book by Gerald R. Ford, member of the Warren Commission, called *Portrait of the Assassin* (1965), raises this question. Ford reprints an Associated Press release dated a week after the Kennedy slaying: "Someone telegraphed small amounts of money to Lee Harvey Oswald for several months before the assassination of President Kennedy, it was reported today. The unidentified sender telegraphed Oswald $10 to $20 at a time."

And Ford comments, "With his background he

could have made a perfect counteragent to spy on Castro's supporters." This comment from a man later to become president of the United States must be considered seriously.

In Texas, the Oswalds, especially Marina, were befriended by Russian-born people living in the area. Most of them were prosperous. They were eager to help a young Russian girl who spoke no English, who had an infant to care for, and whose American husband could not keep a job. Yet after the assassination their doubts about Marina came to the surface.

For example, Gerald Ford reports the testimony of George Bouhe, unofficial leader of the Russian group, before the Warren Commission. Bouhe said: "I think she is a well-brought up girl . . . that she has received good care from some old person of the old regime. Religious, well-mannered, and such.

"She liked glitter, fun, maybe just like any young, pretty girl of that age would, probably, but I think she was also a driver and ambitious about it. . . . And it seems to me that she followed that line by meeting Oswald, coaxing him to come to America, and so, as she told me herself, she could write a postal card to her old friends, 'Watch me sail to America!' "

Bouhe was asked, "You mentioned . . . that you had thought to yourself, 'Isn't it possible that Marina is a great actress?' "

"There again she acts so natural that I was disarmed. But at this stage of the game, maybe I was a fool."

"Why do you say that, Mr. Bouhe?"

"Maybe she is the super-agent of some organization."

Puzzles and Contradictions

The Oswalds lived in Texas for about ten months. They quarreled often — about money, about their life together, about Marina smoking cigarettes and sometimes having a cocktail. Oswald did not approve of smoking or drinking. Sometimes he struck Marina.

During this time, Oswald, using the name of A. J. Hidell, ordered a cheap, Italian-made Mannlicher-Carcano rifle from a mail-order house. The rifle was delivered to his post-office box. Later he acquired a pistol by the same method.

During the Warren investigations, two photos turned up. Marina said she took the snapshots in the spring of 1963. They show Oswald holding the rifle and pistol. But several things seem to be wrong in the pictures. For one, Oswald's body, not his head, seems to be tipped — as though a photo of someone else's body (holding the guns) had been clumsily pasted over Oswald's figure. For another, the flowers seen in the photos are definitely fall flowers.

In May of 1963 the Oswalds were living on unemployment compensation of $33 a week. Lee decided to look for a job in New Orleans. He took a night bus, leaving Marina and June at the home of Mrs. Ruth Paine in the town of Irving, a Dallas suburb.

Ruth Paine, who had two children of her own, was separated from her husband. A student of the Russian language, she wanted to be friends with Marina to practice speaking Russian with her. But this was not the only reason. Ruth Paine sincerely liked Marina and wanted to help her get along in the United States.

Lee got a job in a coffee warehouse. Mrs. Paine drove Marina and June to New Orleans so the Oswalds could be together. In New Orleans Lee soon got himself involved in the politics of the city's Cuban community. But he seems to have switched sides more than once.

To the anti-Castro Cubans, Oswald presented himself as an experienced dynamiter and teacher of guerrilla warfare tactics. Their leader, Carlos Bringuier, was suspicious. On a radio discussion he asked Oswald what he had been doing in the Soviet Union. Oswald replied, "I was under the protection of the American government. . . . I was at all times considered an American citizen."

Oswald and Bringuier later got into a fistfight, and Oswald was thrown into jail. There he asked to see an FBI man. He told the agent he was a pro-Castro fighter, born in Cuba. For some reason, he wanted now to be known publicly as a Castro follower.

He had already identified himself as pro-Castro by setting up a local chapter of the Fair Play for Cuba Committee — with himself as its only member. He even wrote the New York office of the Communist Party: "I stood yesterday . . . with a placard around my neck, passing out Fair Play for Cuba pamphlets. My homemade placards said: HANDS OFF CUBA! VIVA FIDEL!"

Oswald must have known that the FBI read all the Communist Party's mail. Perhaps he wanted to make doubly sure that the FBI heard all about his Fair Play for Cuba capers.

During his New Orleans stay, Oswald apparently wanted to return to Soviet Russia. He applied for a passport and got it, despite his known record of Communist association. Perhaps the passport people only slipped up. Or perhaps they had orders to let Oswald alone.

Marina later claimed that he wanted only to go to Cuba. She said, "I only know that his basic desire was to get to Cuba by any means, and that all the rest of it was window dressing for that purpose."

Fired from his job in August, 1963, Oswald took another step on that twisted journey that was to end forever in Dallas three months later. He left New Orleans for Mexico City. Ruth Paine picked up Marina and June and took them back to her Irving home. Marina was now eight months pregnant with her second child.

In Mexico City, Oswald went to the Cuban Embassy and asked for a visa to Cuba. He said he planned to stop in Cuba on his way to Soviet Russia. The Cubans told him to get his Soviet visa first. But the Soviet Embassy in Mexico City informed him that a Soviet visa would take months. At that time there was no legal, open way to travel directly from the United States to Cuba.

Oswald was reportedly angry at his failure to get a Cuban visa. Perhaps this show of anger was only put on. It is hard to believe that he was acting completely on his own at this time. For one thing, where did he get the money to go from New Orleans to Mexico City?

True, he traveled by bus and stayed at cheap hotels. But he was jobless, and he had a family to support. Was he in the pay of Castro's Cuba? Or was he a double agent, as Gerald Ford suggests — pretending to work for Castro, but in reality in the pay of the United States?

Even if the answer to both these questions is "No way," Cuban intelligence must have had Oswald under observation. It must have watched him in New Orleans and Mexico City. Perhaps it knew about his previous Russian experience as well. It probably traced him on his return to Texas.

Even the Warren Report goes into some detail on Oswald's Cuban connections. It says, "Oswald's activities with regard to Cuba raise serious questions as to how much he might have been motivated in the assassination by a desire to aid the Castro regime." But the Warren Report failed to ask the next logical question: If Oswald helped Cuba, how much help did Cuba give Oswald?

Nor does the Warren Report mention that the CIA was making systematic attempts on the life of Fidel Castro. This did not come to light until 1975, when a U.S. Senate committe began digging. At one point, the CIA hired Chicago gangster Sam Giancana to handle Castro's death. Giancana did not succeed. But when the Senate committee subpoenaed him, he was killed before he could take the stand. Giancana's killer was never caught.

It is not clear that John Kennedy knew about the CIA attempts on Castro's life, and even less clear that he approved. One Kennedy aide later reported that Kennedy wanted no part of a Castro murder. Kennedy is supposed to have said, "If we get into that kind of thing, we'll all be targets."

At least one member of the Warren Commission must have known that the CIA was plotting to kill Castro. He was Allen Dulles, former CIA chief. He was surely aware of what his old outfit was up to. It is obvious, however, that what he knew did not go into the Warren Report. Dulles once admitted that CIA and FBI heads were entitled to lie — if it suited the plans of their organizations — to anybody except the president himself.

And if the CIA kept a running check on Oswald, that record is still secret. It claims no knowledge of his return to Dallas after a week in Mexico City. Marina and little June were living in suburban Irving with Ruth Paine. Mrs. Paine heard of a job opportunity at the Texas School Book Depository and told Oswald about it. He applied and was hired. During the workweek he lived in a Dallas rooming house. He spent weekends with the family in Irving.

About this time the FBI decided to check up on Oswald. A Dallas agent, James P. Hosty, questioned Marina closely about her husband. Enraged, Oswald came to the FBI office early in November and left a note for Hosty. In it he threatened to blow up the office if his wife was bothered again.

Only a few people ever knew about the note until 1975, when Congress began to look into FBI methods. Hosty told the Congressional committee that on the day Oswald was shot, his Dallas boss told him to get rid of the note — as well as all the material in the Oswald file. It may be that the FBI had dealings with Oswald as an undercover agent. It may be that the FBI was trying to deny it knew anything about Oswald at all.

In October, Marina had another daughter, Rachel. It was a bright day in Oswald's life, but he and Marina continued to quarrel. He disapproved of her wanting to be like her American friends. She criticized him for being a poor earner and a poor husband.

In fact, she asked him not to come to Irving on the weekend starting Friday, November 15. Ruth's husband would be there over the weekend, and she feared the two men would clash. Instead, Oswald came to Irving after work on Thursday, November 21.

What Oswald said and did on that evening before the Kennedy assassination is of supreme importance. But nobody actually knows what went on. William Manchester, in *The Death of a President* (1967), says he "went mad." Yet Marina, in her lengthy testimony before the Warren Commission, said that "Lee was not particularly agitated and did not in any particular way reveal his thoughts."

Next morning Oswald arose early and left without breakfast. He went to the nearby home of a fellow worker who customarily drove him to and from Irving, and got in the car. He laid a long, paper-wrapped package on the backseat. Asked about the package, he explained that it contained curtain rods for his Dallas room.

The two drove to the Texas School Book Depository parking lot, and Oswald walked into the building first. No one else noticed him carrying the long package. But when investigators searched the sixth floor after the shooting, they found the wrappings and the Mannlicher-Carcano rifle. They also found three spent shell casings on the floor under the window.

The Warren Commission was convinced from the start that Oswald alone had done the shooting. The commission was thus forced to construct a theory that three bullets, and only three, had done all the damage. One bullet had caved in the back of President Kennedy's head. One bullet had missed entirely, scattering stone and brick fragments that wounded a spectator.

The third bullet was supposed to have entered the back of Kennedy's neck and come through his throat. Then it was supposed to have entered Connally's back, collapsing a lung and breaking ribs, coming out through his rib cage and, finally, shattering his wrist.

Yet this was the bullet found by the side of the stretchers in the Parkland Hospital corridor. This was the bullet that bore little or no trace of all the injury it was supposed to have caused. This is the Magic Bullet that upsets the neat theory of the Warren Commission.

Was it possible for a bullet to have done so much harm and yet end up almost unmarked? Was there another bullet, another gun — another marksman?

There have been attempts to prove that the bullet hole in Kennedy's throat was an entrance wound rather than an exit wound. This would mean that the second killer was firing from in front of SS 100X, rather than from behind and above, where Oswald was stationed.

Detailed studies of the Zapruder film have been made. These tend to show that Kennedy reacted to the bullet by jerking backward, as if hit in the throat. Or did the back brace he always wore for his old injury jerk him backwards in reaction to a bullet from the rear?

The Zapruder film offers an exact timing of the three shots. But could a Mannlicher-Carcano rifle, cheaply and poorly made, be fired that fast? Tests have been inconclusive. And, being fired that fast, could such a rifle have scored two hits out of three? Accuracy tests have also been inconclusive.

Complicating the argument is the story of Jack Ruby, the man who killed Oswald. Was he, too, supposed to have been acting alone? Was he merely an unstable personality who responded to a sudden impulse and shot Oswald — as the Warren Report indicates? Or was he a part, a still-unexplained part, of the conspiracy?

Ruby was a nightclub operator who liked to make friends with Dallas policemen. Friendly officers were entertained free at his nightclub. In turn they allowed Ruby to break the law in small ways. This gave Ruby a sense of self-importance. So did the revolver and the large sums of cash he always carried.

Ruby needed this feeling of being a big shot. He was born in the Chicago slums. His father deserted the family early, and his mother spent long periods in mental hospitals. Ruby grew up involved in illegal, fast-buck schemes, always on the fringe of crime. After World War II service, he came to Dallas and began running nightclubs.

Unmarried, Ruby was almost insanely devoted to his dogs. He called them his "family," his "children." And he seemed to grieve deeply over President Kennedy's death. Ruby's behavior during those forty-six hours between Kennedy's and Oswald's slayings has been closely studied. What comes out is a pattern of emotional upset that may have led to the crime.

But there are several unanswered questions in Ruby's history. They tend to deny that he shot Oswald in a sudden fit. One question deals with the fact that Ruby had been an FBI informer. Another question concerns Ruby's attempts to sell Castro a fleet of U.S. Army jeeps. Ruby had been in Havana right after the Castro takeover, and knew many people who helped Castro to power.

Closer to home, Ruby had been at that Friday midnight press conference in which Oswald protested his innocence. And after his arrest, Ruby pleaded with Chief Justice Warren to be taken to Washington. Only there, away from Dallas, would it be safe for Ruby to reveal important information. Or so Ruby said.

But Ruby was never allowed to leave Dallas. He was tried and convicted for Oswald's murder. While awaiting an appeal on his sentence, he died of cancer. Whatever important information he possessed died with him.

Oswald is dead. Ruby is dead. A number of others, whose stories might have helped answer the conspiracy charges, are dead, too. Many of them died silently, violently, before their time, and their deaths go unexplained.

Even President Lyndon Johnson, who set up the Warren Commission, had his doubts. In a 1969 interview he said, "I can't honestly say that I've ever been completely relieved of the fact that there might have been international connections."

Senator from New York

For months after Dallas, Robert Kennedy was numbed by sorrow. He returned to his desk as head of the Justice Department, but he could not keep his mind on his work. He stared into space. His thoughts wandered. Many times he left his work to be with his brother's children. Other times he went home in the middle of the day to be with his own family.

Rose Kennedy, always strong, consoled everyone. Joe Kennedy had been felled by a stroke two years before. A speechless invalid, he could not communicate even by writing. Yet his mind was still clear, and now very grieved. Ted, elected U.S. senator from Massachusetts in 1962, was a source of silent strength.

At the 1963 Justice Department's Christmas party for poor children, something happened that tested Bob's emotional control. Seeing him, a child — about six years old — blurted out, "Your brother's dead!" The room fell silent, and the little boy began to cry. Bob dropped to his knees and put his arms around the child. "That's all right," he said. "I have another brother."

By spring Robert Kennedy began to face forward. President Johnson was sure to run next November, and his chances for election were excellent. People wondered what Bob would do. He might ask for reappointment as attorney general. He might seek some other public post, perhaps as ambassador to the United Nations or to the Soviet Union. He might become a teacher or a writer.

Gradually Bob decided that he wanted to stay in public life — and that he could best serve as vice president. In that post he could help Johnson carry out John Kennedy's program. In the back of his mind, of course, was the idea that when Johnson stepped down, say in 1972, he would run for president himself.

President Johnson had other ideas. A proud man, Johnson wanted to throw off the Kennedy influence and become his own president. He felt, rightly or wrongly, that Robert Kennedy as vice president would overshadow him. But he couldn't say "No" right to Kennedy's face. So he told his whole cabinet that he would not consider any of them as his vice presidential running mate.

Robert Kennedy played a prominent part at the

Democratic National Convention held in August, 1964, at Atlantic City. His role was to speak briefly about John F. Kennedy and to show a film about his brother's life called *Years of Lightning, Days of Drums*. Talking calmly about the slain president, Bob showed his sorrow only once. That was when he quoted from Shakespeare's *Romeo and Juliet:*

When he shall die take him out and cut him out into stars, and he shall make the face of heaven so fine that all the world will be in love with night and pay no worship to the garish sun.

Bob ended his talk by reminding the convention of its duty to keep on with the program that John Kennedy had started. Then he gave the closing lines to Robert Frost's "Stopping by Woods on a Snowy Evening," a favorite of his brother's:

The woods are lovely, dark, and deep
But I have promises to keep
And miles to go before I sleep
And miles to go before I sleep.

The convention wept over and cheered this remembrance of their lost leader. Many wished that a Kennedy was still in — or near — the White House.

Robert Kennedy was a practical man, however. He knew now that he could not run as Johnson's junior partner. He had to win election to public office on his own.

New York State Democrats were looking for a candidate to oppose Republican Kenneth Keating in the race for U.S. senator. After much backstage maneuvering, they nominated Robert Kennedy.

Kennedy had lived in New York as a boy, but his real roots were in Massachusetts. His family had been in Massachusetts for four generations. Teddy was U.S. senator from that state.

Many New Yorkers didn't want an out-of-stater as their senatorial candidate (although the U.S. Constitution requires only that a senator be living in the state at the time of his election). A *New York Times* editorial asked, "Mr. Kennedy needs New York, but does New York really need Mr. Kennedy?"

Among other names, Bob was called a "carpetbagger" — a word first used to describe the fortune-hunting Northerners who moved into the stricken South right after the Civil War ended. Many carried luggage made out of carpet strips. To shake off the charge, Bob took a house in Glen Cove, Long Island, and later an apartment in New York City.

He also had to shake off the charge that he was "ruthless." This came from the days when he was savagely pursuing labor leader Jimmy Hoffa. It also came from his drive to get his brother elected. Later, columnist Joseph Alsop wrote, "So many people have him absolutely wrong. They think he is cold, calculating, ruthless. Actually he is hot-blooded, romantic, compassionate."

Bob Kennedy showed his real nature in the campaign. He was patient, even-tempered, and showed a genuine liking for people. He stood on hundreds of street corners, answering questions and listening to complaints.

Of course Kennedy hitched his own campaign to Lyndon Johnson's. When the votes were in, Johnson had carried New York State by a margin of two and one-half million votes. Kennedy beat Keating by 720,000 votes. So, in one sense, Kennedy rode to victory on Johnson's coattails. In another sense, he proved that he could really win an election, that he didn't have to be appointed to office by someone else.

In winning, Bob Kennedy proved something more. A year after his brother's death, he proved that he had mastered his grief and was able to move forward. He never forgot his brother, but he never allowed his anguish to slow him down again.

U.S. Senator Robert Kennedy had to learn a new kind of politicking. As attorney general, he had been his own boss. He set up goals and proceeded toward them in a fairly straight line.

As senator, the voters were his boss. His goals — if attained at all — were reached by a zigzag route. He had to compromise, to agree with both sides in an argument. He had to see that all voters got at least a part of what they demanded. And he learned to wait — while committees met and congressmen went home to run for reelection.

Example: His fight to control cigarette sales. Bob Kennedy had a special interest in young people. He realized early that cigarette ads were helping to coax half a million teenagers every year to start smoking. In 1964, the year he was elected, the Surgeon General of the United States issued an important official statement. It said that smoking was unhealthy, and something must be done about it.

Soon Bob Kennedy became a leader in the anti-smoking battle. Against him were the cigarette manufacturers, the ad agencies, the radio and TV networks, even the airlines, which were paid to pass out free cigarettes to passengers. Kennedy tried hard to get the cigarette companies to quit pushing their product on teenagers.

He wanted them to stop picturing smoking as romantic or manly. He wanted them to stop running commercials on TV sports broadcasts. He worked for a cigarette tax based on how much nicotine and tar the tobacco contained. He fought for a stronger warning printed on the cigarette package.

For years the cigarette industry refused to listen. Only in the late 1960's did it begin to submit to the rules he wanted.

The anti-smoking struggle was only one example of Kennedy's involvement with youth, notably poor black youth. At first he thought more and better education was the answer to the black problem.

When he was attorney general he helped set up the Model School Program in a black area of the District of Columbia. Textbooks written about and for suburban white children were thrown out. Materials that meant something to poor black kids were adopted. Ex-Peace Corps instructors and others who knew how to reach the disadvantaged were brought in. Soon the black children were learning more.

But as a senator, Kennedy became convinced that giving blacks a good education was just not enough. Even well-educated blacks could not always better their lives. Only a few could get the kinds of jobs they had studied for. These truths were bloodily emphasized in the Watts riot of 1965.

Watts is an all-black community set off by itself in Los Angeles. At the time it was a neglected area. It offered few jobs. It had poor housing, poor police and fire protection, poor bus transportation, poor garbage collection.

In August, 1965, Watts exploded for seven days. The burning, wrecking, and looting were finally stopped by police and soldiers.

The whole of America watched the rioting on TV. Many people feared that the same thing could break out in their own neighborhoods. Other people asked, "What caused it? What can we do to prevent another Watts?"

One answer was "law and order" — stronger and swifter police action. Bob Kennedy was not promoting mob violence, nor was he condemning prompt police action. But he was against certain laws. He criticized the law that permitted a black's paycheck to be seized for an unpaid debt. He fought the law that permitted a white merchant to cheat a black customer. These were the laws, he said, that helped spark the Watts riot.

Yet Kennedy was more interested in cures than in causes. What could help cure the black problem? School integration and better education did not seem to work. He decided that the answer lay in jobs.

But private industry could not hire hundreds of thousands of blacks overnight. Many labor unions were not ready to accept large numbers of new black members. And many blacks had never been able to go to trade schools or get on-the-job training. They could do little better than unskilled labor. Where were the jobs for all these unemployed?

One solution: Put them to work rebuilding the black ghettos. Many black communities were (and some still are) a disgrace and an eyesore. Many of the dwellings were rotten, stinking firetraps. Many school buildings were shabby and worn, with outdated classroom equipment and no real cafeterias, gyms, playgrounds. Few black neighborhoods had adequate parks or community centers.

There were many such ghettos — Watts, New York's Harlem, Chicago's South Side. To start, Kennedy chose the Bedford-Stuyvesant district in

Brooklyn, New York. (Brooklyn is one of the five boroughs that make up New York City.)

In the mid-1960's, "Bed-Stuy" was ready to go up in flames. It had about 300,000 people, mostly black or Spanish-speaking. Too many of its houses were about to fall apart. Too many of its workers were unemployed. Too many of its young people were not in school. Too many of its infants were dying.

Kennedy couldn't just say to Bed-Stuy: "Here's some money, some materials, some tools. Fix yourself up." His plan needed to involve the federal, state, and city governments. It had to get loans from banks and investment companies, and assistance from industry. It needed help from labor unions and from vocational schools. It had to win the aid of the Bed-Stuy leaders — politicians, heads of community organizations, church officials.

Everything took time, and by 1968 the work had scarcely begun. But at Robert Kennedy's death, the Bed-Stuy planners started moving. Today Bedford-Stuyvesant, still largely unfinished, is beginning to show the effort and the result.

And many people still remember what Robert Kennedy once said: "If I could do what I really wanted to do, I would resign from the Senate and run Bedford-Stuyvesant."

The Kennedys and Vietnam

Vietnam is a long strip of hilly country running along the east coast of the Indochina Peninsula. It faces the South China Sea, guarding the vital shipping lanes between China and India. For a thousand years foreign nations fought for control of this strategic location.

In the late 1700's France began to take over Vietnam. By 1900 almost the whole peninsula was under the French. Japan long wanted French Indochina, and seized it at the start of World War II. When the Japanese were finally defeated in 1945, a native Vietnamese group called the Vietminh set up a government in the land.

The returning French put in their own government, and a long civil war broke out. The Vietminh gradually admitted that they were Communists. After years of guerrilla warfare, the Vietminh inflicted a punishing defeat on the French at Dienbienphu in 1954.

The defeat forced France to give Vietnam its independence. The postwar agreement divided the land in half. North Vietnam — the Democratic Republic of Vietnam — was Communist. South Vietnam — the Republic of Vietnam — had a democratic form of government.

The agreement also provided for free elections to be held in South Vietnam. Backed by the United States, the South Vietnam government would not permit the elections to be held. Both countries feared that the Communists would win the elections and take over the country.

Congressman John Kennedy, accompanied by Bob and their sister Patricia, had visited Vietnam (still one country then) on their global tour in 1951. John Kennedy saw that communism was already reaching into southern Vietnam.

After Vietnam was split into two countries, Kennedy warned that South Vietnam was still not free. Many of its people teetered towards communism, he said. And he noted the influence of China, a Communist power next door.

Kennedy believed that no amount of outside military help could throw communism out of South Vietnam as long as it had the sympathy and undercover support of the South Vietnamese. The United States simply could not go in by itself, face both China and the unwilling South Vietnamese, and expect to win.

John Kennedy never really changed his mind about South Vietnam. When he became president he began to help the South Vietnamese fight their own battles against communism. Their major enemies were the Vietcong. Some Vietcong had infiltrated down from North Vietnam. Other Vietcong were South Vietnamese Communists. Supplies and arms came chiefly from North Vietnam — which was supplied by China and the Soviet Union.

By November, 1963, President Kennedy had sent about 16,300 military men to South Vietnam. These included advisers and instructors, helicopter teams, and 600 Special Forces ("Green Berets") to train and lead the South Vietnamese in guerrilla warfare.

But Kennedy always refused to be trapped into an all-out war with North Vietnam. As late as September 2, 1963, less than three months before he was killed, he said of the South Vietnamese: ". . . it is their war. They are the ones who have to win it or lose it. We can help them, we can give them equipment, we can send our men out there as advisers, but they have to win it. . . ."

This did not mean that John Kennedy wanted to withdraw American aid. It did mean he was putting limits on the American involvement in Vietnam.

The picture began to change after Lyndon Johnson became president. At first Johnson vowed that he would not send "American boys to fight in Asia's wars." Nevertheless he stepped up U.S. forces, including air and naval units, in the Vietnam area.

Then in August, 1964, two U.S. destroyers were cruising in the Gulf of Tonkin off the North Vietnam and South China coasts. The destroyers were supposedly attacked by North Vietnamese patrol boats. They returned fire and sank two of the boats. Many critics of the Vietnam war doubt that any of this actually happened.

Whether it did or not, President Johnson carried the story to Congress. Congress voted him a Gulf of Tonkin Resolution. This gave him a blank check to expand the American part in the Vietnam war.

From that point, it was all uphill. More than a half million U.S. military men were sent to Vietnam. U.S. planes dropped more bombs on North Vietnam than had been used against Germany in World War II.

However, neither U.S. nor South Vietnamese ground troops ever invaded North Vietnam. Instead they fought in the hills, jungles, and rice paddies of the southern half of the peninsula. Casualties were high on both sides. By the end of the war, about 56,000 Americans had lost their lives.

Even though the Vietnam war went on year after year, a majority of the American people backed Johnson's war policies. But a strong minority strongly disagreed. This minority protested in many ways — in parades and demonstrations, in raids on draft offices, in public draft-card burnings, in desertions from the Armed Forces.

For a long time Robert Kennedy agreed with Johnson on the war. He said, "The United States has made a commitment to help Vietnam. I'm in favor of keeping that commitment and taking whatever steps are necessary."

But the war kept on escalating. More and more U.S. bombs were dropped. More and more men on both sides were killed. Young U.S. officers, eager to please their superiors, turned in exaggerated "body counts" — the number of enemy slain in battle. Adding up these body counts, the whole enemy force would have been wiped out early on in the war.

Robert Kennedy finally joined the protestors. One of the men who helped turn him against our involvement in Vietnam was Pierre Mendes-France, former French premier. Mendes-France had seen his country defeated at Dienbienphu, and he knew the uselessness of fighting such a foe:

The mobile war of the jungle and the mountains is their way. They know they can beat you at it. You may win the pitched battles, but you will not win the country. The Vietcong will die in the paddies, fade into the jungles, but they or others will return and reclaim what you think you have won. The people are not with you.

Almost from the beginning of the war, both sides extended — and withdrew — peace feelers. There were bombing halts, combat truces, and secret meetings that came to nothing. In time the Johnson Administration gave up hoping it was going to win a total military victory. It was willing to accept a negotiated peace. Trouble was, who was the United States willing to negotiate with?

Would it deal only with North Vietnam? Or would the Vietcong and their political arm, the National Liberation Front (NLF), also sit at the bargaining table? And sitting there, would the Communist-run NLF then have a right to be part of the postwar South Vietnamese government?

Those were the questions that finally split Robert Kennedy away from Lyndon Johnson. Kennedy believed that the Vietcong-NLF had a right to sit in on the peace negotiations. Johnson did not. Further, Johnson felt that the only way to force the enemy to begin peace talks was to intensify the bombing. Kennedy wanted a bombing halt. The two argued angrily.

Yet Kennedy postponed any move to make himself a candidate for the presidency. He was sure that Johnson would run again, and win again, in 1968. However, another Democrat was ready to make his bid for the office. He was Eugene McCarthy, U.S. senator from Minnesota.

McCarthy was a new breed of politician. He was low-key, thoughtful, an intellectual — very different from the loud, "press the flesh" hand-shaker Johnson. McCarthy was different, too, from the hard-driving, intense Robert Kennedy. But he shared Kennedy's Catholic faith. And he shared his opposition to the war.

McCarthy might have gone almost unnoticed except for a sudden upset in the course of the Vietnam fighting. Ever since the war began, U.S. generals kept on saying that the enemy was weakening and the war would soon be over. High U.S. officials visited Vietnam, studied the scene for a few days, and said the same thing. Then came January, 1968 — and Tet.

Tet is the Vietnamese holiday season that occurs at the Lunar New Year. Both sides had always declared a Tet truce of several days. Soldiers went home or celebrated in camp.

But in 1968 the enemy forces disregarded the Tet truce. They struck with sudden fury at cities all over South Vietnam. In the capital city of Saigon they boldly raided the American Embassy to show their reach and power. It was a stunning demonstration of force. It was clear proof that they were as strong as ever, ready to fight on.

After Tet, many Americans felt they had been fooled for years by their government and its experts. They showed their loss of faith in a quiet but effective way. In March, 1968, New Hampshire held its presidential primary, the first state in the nation to do so. New Hampshire Democrats gave 42.2 percent of their vote to newcomer Eugene McCarthy.

As a president running for renomination, Lyndon Johnson should have won most of the votes.

Earlier presidents running for renomination had always done so, even without campaigning. It was a clear signal to Johnson that the country was not behind him.

On March 31, President Johnson did two important things. Over nationwide TV he called for a bombing halt. He also said, "I shall not seek and I will not accept the nomination of my party for another term as your president."

In the Running

The Tet offensive changed Robert Kennedy's mind about running for president. Now he wanted it. He saw himself fighting Johnson for the nomination, with the Vietnam war as the issue between them. But he agonized over his decision to run. The result was that he acted too late to enter the New Hampshire primary.

Instead, the New Hampshire primary made Eugene McCarthy the most talked-about politician in America. Kennedy took a backseat. And when Johnson dropped out of the race, Kennedy floundered even more. With Johnson out, who was Kennedy going to run against? He had no real quarrel with McCarthy.

So he decided to run, not against somebody but against something — the war that was tearing America apart. To be sure, if he won the nomination he'd face a formidable Republican foe. Richard Nixon was certain to get the nod from his party. And Nixon, Kennedy felt, was in no hurry to end the Vietnam war.

In deciding to run, Bob Kennedy asked the advice of a number of experts. Some told him to run, some to wait. Earlier polls, however, had showed him to be the public's first choice for the nomination: Young people were for him. So were the poor. The man on the street liked Kennedy.

But a surprising number now backed Eugene McCarthy. He, too, had a following among youth. In fact, he recruited many young campaign workers for the New Hampshire primary. Many of them cut their hair, put on ties and jackets, and proclaimed themselves to be "Clean for Gene."

What's more, a number of professional Democratic politicians were either for McCarthy or postponing a choice. Kennedy knew his strength was with the people, not the party pros. That's why he made up his mind to enter several primaries — to prove to the Democratic National Convention that the people wanted him.

Kennedy entered the contest without a real organization. This was in contrast to the well-disciplined campaign army he had enlisted for his brother in 1960. He entered late — there was time only to run in a few states. And he entered under a load of criticism — that he had let McCarthy knock Johnson out of the race, that he was running on his brother's name and reputation, and so on.

Indiana was Robert Kennedy's first primary. His opponents were McCarthy and the state governor, Roger Branigin. McCarthy was the only real threat.

The campaign had scarcely begun when, on April 4, Dr. Martin Luther King was assassinated in Memphis. The murder took place just before Kennedy was scheduled to speak at a ghetto rally in Indianapolis. Kennedy was again reminded that death was always chillingly close. He announced the tragedy to the audience in an impassioned outburst:

For those of you who are black and are tempted to be filled with hatred and distrust at the injustice of such an act, against all white people, I can only say I feel in my heart the same kind of feeling. I had a member of my family killed . . . But we have to make an effort . . . to understand, to go beyond these difficult times. My favorite poet was Aeschylus. He wrote: "Even in our sleep, pain which cannot forget falls drop by drop upon the heart until in our own despair against our will, comes wisdom through the awful grace of God."

What we need in the United States is not division . . . not hatred . . . not violence or lawlessness, but love and wisdom and compassion toward one another, and a feeling of justice toward those who still suffer within our country, whether they be white . . . or black.

That same night Kennedy met with fourteen black leaders. They were bitter over King's death and suspicious of Kennedy. He told them: "I have only one thing to offer you — my word. I want and need your help. I wanted Martin Luther King's help, and he gave me his help, not only to me but to other white people who were trying to help his people."

The black leaders set aside their anger and promised to support Robert Kennedy.

Kennedy campaigned in Indiana for two weeks. One of his best tours was a train trip along the route of the Wabash Cannonball in central Indiana. Crowds gathered at every stop to hear him speak informally from the back platform of the train. He also toured the state by car, speaking, answering questions, shaking hands early and late.

Kennedy won the Indiana primary, but not by very much. He was heartened, however, by his strong support from both black and lower-middle-income white voters. These two groups rarely back the same candidate.

In Nebraska, his second primary state, Kennedy had the help of two important Nebraskans. One was Ted Sorensen, one of John Kennedy's top aides. The other was Ted's brother Phil, formerly lieutenant governor of the state. Speaking to large crowds, Kennedy offered the people what they wanted to hear: a Vietnam slowdown and good farm price supports.

Nebraska gave Kennedy a majority of its vote.

But Hubert Humphrey was coming up fast. Vice president under Johnson, he had entered the race when Johnson dropped out. (Humphrey won the 1968 Democratic nomination and lost the general election to Richard Nixon by only a narrow margin.)

Next stop: Oregon. Here Robert Kennedy was in trouble. He had no organization in the state, and no time to set one up. And Oregon was white, prosperous, and not inclined to listen to Kennedy's crisis-type of campaigning. McCarthy had more appeal for Oregonians.

McCarthy challenged Kennedy to a TV debate. He refused, and McCarthy used his refusal in a powerful radio and TV commercial: "He wouldn't stand up to Johnson in New Hampshire. Now he won't stand up to McCarthy in Oregon."

Very little seemed to go right for Kennedy in the Oregon race. When the votes were counted, McCarthy came out a clear winner.

Kennedy had his hopes set on a more important victory, the upcoming California race. Even during the Oregon campaign, he stole time to make speeches and shake hands in California. He was counting on the California voters to speak for the whole country.

On the morning after his Oregon loss, Kennedy talked to newsmen in Los Angeles. Now he blasted Humphrey: "If the vice president is nominated to oppose Richard Nixon, there will be no candidate who has opposed the . . . war in Vietnam. There will be no candidate committed to . . . remedy [ing] the conditions which are transforming our cities into armed camps."

McCarthy, fresh from his Oregon victory, was still very much in the race. He stepped up his advertising campaign against Kennedy. One full-page ad in the *Los Angeles Times* read: "Eugene McCarthy was the first man to cry out 'Let the killing stop,' and he was the first man with guts to add 'Why are we there?' "

The truth perhaps was that McCarthy was the first *declared* candidate to say these things. Kennedy, who had announced his candidacy later than McCarthy, had been outspokenly anti-Vietnam for nearly two years.

Nevertheless, Kennedy was hugely popular in California. Crowds surged around him every place he went. They grabbed his outstretched hands, tore away at his clothes. He lost countless cufflinks and *PT-109* tie clasps.

Kennedy appealed most to white liberals, to blacks and Mexican-Americans, and to young people who followed a different lifestyle. But he did not neglect the conservatives and the elderly. To them he emphasized his experience as an efficient attorney general. He spoke proudly of his ability to serve as president of all the people.

In the whirlwind campaigns before California, Kennedy had left his wife and children behind at Hickory Hill. Now he wanted his family near him, to sustain his spirit and give him the strength to continue. So Ethel and six of the children joined him in the last days of the California campaign.

With his family beside him, Kennedy found time for a little fun and frolic. On the Sunday afternoon before Election Day (Tuesday, June 4), they all went to Disneyland. They whooped and hollered, their father enjoying himself most of all.

Election Day was spent swimming at Malibu Beach. Robert Kennedy returned early in the evening to his campaign suite at the Ambassador Hotel in Los Angeles. South Dakota was also holding its primary elections that day. Although Kennedy had not campaigned there, he was on its ballot. Early returns indicated that he would get about 50 percent of the Democratic vote. This pleased him, for Hubert Humphrey had been born in South Dakota and should have taken the biggest vote.

The suite was thronged with campaign aides and personal friends. Among them were two black friends of the candidate, Roosevelt (Rosie) Grier, former top pro football player, and Rafer Johnson, former Olympic decathlon champion. Everyone was cheering the TV reports of mounting Kennedy totals in California and South Dakota. They talked of the next campaign in New York, and what special appeals had to be made to the state which Kennedy represented as senator.

It was close to midnight when Kennedy went down to the hotel ballroom to give the traditional victory speech to his assembled campaign workers. In a short talk he was both humorous and grateful to the workers. He was full of renewed energy for the road ahead, the road to the Democratic nomination for president.

In a few minutes that road would disappear.

A Second Death,
a Second Slayer

It was after midnight when Robert Kennedy finished his speech. The campaign workers gathered around him, chanting, "We want Bobbie! We want Bobbie!" Newsmen shouting questions pushed mikes into his face. Cameramen shot pictures of him from every angle. He had won the California primary, and he looked like the next president.

A security guard, trying to shake off the clamoring throng, led Kennedy through double doors into the hotel's serving pantry. Kennedy stopped to greet the kitchen workers. Then it happened.

A short, slight, dark-complexioned young man came up close to the senator. He drew a gun, later identified as a .22-caliber pistol, and began shooting at Kennedy.

By the time he had fired the second or third shot, the gunman was grabbed and wrestled down.

Nevertheless, he kept on firing until the pistol was empty. Five people around the senator were hit, too.

Robert Kennedy had been wounded three times. It was plain to see that he was close to death. The happy confusion after his victory speech turned into the wildest chaos. The crowd was yelling, screaming for a doctor, for the police, weeping over the shooting. The serving pantry became a nightmare setting.

A few remained calm. Ethel Kennedy, three months pregnant with her eleventh child, knelt and held her husband's hand. Jesse Unruh, California political leader, kept the crowd from the young gunman. "We don't want another Oswald," he repeated. He meant that the assailant, unlike Lee Harvey Oswald, should live to be tried for his crime.

Eventually an ambulance arrived to take Kennedy to a hospital. At once doctors began probing to find the extent of the injury. One bullet had entered behind his right ear on the way to his brain. It was decided to move the gravely wounded man to another hospital for surgery. There the Kennedy group waited anxiously in a room near the operating room.

Thousands of others waited silently outside the hospital. President Johnson was notified. He alerted cabinet members and key government officials. Ted Kennedy phoned Hyannisport. Jacqueline Kennedy flew from New York in the first plane she could catch.

The surgeons worked all night. Their report was not hopeful. Even if Kennedy were to live, he would be seriously and permanently disabled. Bulletins were issued every few hours for the rest of the day. They offered no encouragement.

Finally press secretary Frank Mankiewicz came into the pressroom and announced, "Senator Robert Francis Kennedy died at 1:44 A.M. today, June 6, 1968." The waiting was over. And as it did for John Kennedy five years before, the nation went into mourning.

The White House sent the presidential jet to carry the body to New York. Funeral services were to be held at St. Patrick's Cathedral on Fifth Avenue. A huge crowd met the plane at LaGuardia Airport at nine that night.

More crowds had surrounded St. Patrick's by the time the coffin was brought to the cathedral. Even though the doors would not open until 5:30 the next morning, people began lining up in the streets. They stood all night in order to walk past the bier and pay their last respects.

June 7, a day of deep grieving, was a hot day in New York. Tens of thousands filed through the cathedral's soaring arches and up to the transept. There the coffin was circled by tall candles. Friends of Robert Kennedy, among them the nation's brightest and best, took turns standing vigil. The mourning public did not halt their silent parade until five the next morning.

Services were held on June 8. The cathedral was filled with 2,300 invited guests. President Johnson and Chief Justice Warren were there. So was Mrs. Martin Luther King, her husband slain only two months before.

Teddy said of his brother:

He gave us strength in time of trouble, wisdom in time of uncertainty, and sharing in times of happiness. . . . He loved life completely and he lived it intensely. . . . My brother need not be idealized, or enlarged in death beyond what he was in life, to be remembered simply as a good and decent man, who saw wrong and tried to right it, saw suffering and tried to heal it, saw war and tried to stop it.

Ted closed his eulogy by quoting the words of playwright George Bernard Shaw. Robert Kennedy had often used these words to end his own campaign speeches: "Some men see things as they are and say 'Why?' I dream things that never were and say 'Why not?' "

Robert Kennedy was to be buried next to John Kennedy at Arlington Cemetery. A 21-car train carried the coffin and nearly a thousand family members and friends from New York to Washington. The train left New York's Penn Station and moved slowly along the 226-mile route. At every town along the way, great numbers gathered to bid a last farewell to Robert Kennedy. Ethel and her eldest son, Joe III, now fifteen, walked through the train and thanked people for their devotion.

In Washington, cars and a bus were waiting to transport the funeral party to Arlington. The procession made a short stop at the Lincoln Memorial. Then it stopped at Resurrection City, a temporary encampment of poor blacks who had come to Washington to protest. Many of these people had regarded Robert Kennedy as their only white friend.

It was night when the motorcade reached the burial ground. Mourners held candles to light the way for the pallbearers. The American flag draped on the coffin was folded, and astronaut John Glenn carried it to Ted Kennedy. He gave it to Ethel. President Johnson watched silently. The ceremony was soon over. The mourners retreated slowly from the graves of Robert and John Kennedy.

On the other side of the continent, the young gunman had been taken to Los Angeles' Rampart Street police station. There he was searched. Four $100 bills, several miscellaneous items, and a clipping of a newspaper column were found in his pocket. The columnist had criticized Kennedy for opposing the war in Vietnam while advocating help for Israel.

The prisoner had no identification. He would not tell his name or anything about himself. Soon he was taken downtown to police headquarters at Parker Center. There he was photographed, fingerprinted, and booked on the charge of assault with intent to commit murder.

Bit by bit his story came out. His name was Sirhan (pronounced "seer-hahn") Bishara Sirhan. He was twenty-four (the same age Oswald had been in November, 1963). A Palestinian Arab, he had been born in what was then the Jordanian part of the city of Jerusalem.

In 1957 his father brought his family to Los Angeles but, unable to adjust to American ways, he soon returned alone to the Middle East. The mother and five children were left to shift for themselves. They managed to get along, partly on welfare, partly on their own earnings.

Sirhan was graduated from a Los Angeles high school and attended junior college for a few terms. After he left school, he got a job exercising race horses. He wanted to be a jockey. But he was thrown from a horse and suffered a head injury. Thereafter he did no regular work.

His insurance claim for the head injury was settled for about $1700. With that, plus money from odd jobs, he kept himself alive financially by betting on horse races. He did well enough to drive a used DeSoto, to date girls, and to tour the taverns with his male friends.

He also found time to read the newspapers, especially about the Middle East. And it was the Middle East issue that drove him to murder Robert

Kennedy. At least that's what students of Sirhan's behavior at the time decided.

As a Palestinian Arab, Sirhan became convinced that Israel was treating his people harshly. He did not consider that Israel was fighting for its own existence, that the whole Arab world had vowed "to drive Israel into the sea." He did not consider that Israel had given its own Arab citizens full rights. He saw only the plight of the Palestinian Arabs. They had fled Israel when that nation was founded in 1947. They were still without a country of their own.

Sirhan's hate for Israel grew more and more intense. It became an obsession with him, perhaps aggravated by his head injury. He bottled up his grievances inside himself.

Sirhan followed the news of Robert Kennedy with interest. At first he liked Kennedy for his attention to the underdogs of every kind. But when Kennedy spoke in favor of selling planes to Israel, Sirhan's liking turned to fury. He obtained a pistol, lay in wait for Kennedy, and killed him.

At Sirhan's trial, his lawyers tried to plead that the crime was "murder in the second degree" — he was not completely responsible because of his Palestinian Arab background and his head injury. But the court ruled that he had committed "murder in the first degree" — he was fully responsible for his act. Sirhan was sentenced to die in the gas chamber.

Before the sentence could be carried out, the U.S. Supreme Court outlawed the death penalty for most crimes. Sirhan's sentence was changed to life imprisonment. Some day he may be considered for parole.

For several years after the Robert Kennedy murder, most critics were satisfied that Sirhan had been a lone gunman acting out his tortured passions. But when the various conspiracy theories in the John Kennedy killing came up, people also took a new look at the slaying of his brother.

For example, Sirhan's .22-caliber pistol had room for just eight bullets. Critics now argue that more than eight shots were fired. Investigations are under way to back up that argument. Even at the time of Sirhan's arrest, there was talk of a companion, maybe a woman, with him at the hotel. Renewed attempts are being made to track down that companion.

Other critics now question whether the Middle East issue really triggered Sirhan's act. They say that Sirhan could have been backed by any number of Kennedy-haters. These include the mobsters and labor-union racketeers that Kennedy chased in the late 1950's and as attorney general. They include the anti-black and anti-Mexican-American people enraged at Kennedy's attention to these minorities. They include both pro-Castro and anti-Castro Cubans. The pro-Castroites claim that Kennedy plotted to murder their leader. The anti-

Castro people charge that Kennedy failed them at the Bay of Pigs.

In 1975 the Kennedy family asked that no further probe be made into the murder of the two brothers. Nothing more was to be gained, they said, by digging deeper into the crimes. They wanted the healing hand of time to do its work.

Did the Kennedy family have a right to make this request?

Epilogue:
The Search Must Go On

In one sense, the Kennedy family has every right to ask that the investigations cease. If they no longer wish to learn who the true killers were, why should the public be so hot on the trail? After all, John and Robert Kennedy belonged first to their family. It should be up to the remaining Kennedys to continue, or to call off, the hunt.

It must be very painful for the Kennedys to keep going over and over the murder stories. They want the wounds to heal; they want to forget; they want to live in the present, not the past. The Kennedy children should be allowed to grow up without the tragedies always before them.

Teddy Kennedy is often proposed as a Democratic candidate for the presidency. Public opinion polls show him to be a likely winner. But the last Kennedy brother says that he doesn't want to run.

He says that he must take care of his brothers' families as well as his own. And, although he has never really said so in public, he must fear the bullets of another assassin, acting alone or in conspiracy.

Ted Kennedy has good reason to be afraid. Several American presidents have been marked for slaying. Some killers have succeeded. In 1975 Lynette Fromme and then Sara Jane Moore each tried to shoot President Gerald Ford. They were the first women to attempt directly to assassinate a president, but they were only the latest on the list of real or would-be slayers of presidents.

The attempts began in 1835, when Richard Lawrence fired two shots at President Andrew Jackson. Jackson escaped unharmed. Thirty years later, actor John Wilkes Booth killed Abraham Lincoln as the president watched a play at Ford's Theater in Washington, D.C.

Charles J. Guiteau fatally shot President James Garfield in 1881. The president had been on his way to board a train in a Washington depot. Twenty years after the Garfield slaying, Leon Czolgosz fired a pistol at President William McKinley at a reception in Buffalo, New York. McKinley died eight days later.

Ex-President Theodore Roosevelt had been out of office for four years when he decided to run again in 1912. He was making a speech in Milwaukee when John N. Schrank seriously wounded him with a revolver shot. Roosevelt recovered.

President-elect Franklin Roosevelt was speaking in Miami in 1933. Guiseppe Zangara opened fire, missing Roosevelt but hitting five people nearby. Anton J. Cermak, mayor of Chicago, died of the wounds he received.

One afternoon in 1950, President Harry Truman was napping upstairs at Blair House, the temporary White House. Two terrorists, Oscar Collazo and Greselio Torresola, tried to break in. Torresola was slain and Collazo seriously wounded in the try. Policeman Leslie Coffelt was killed in the gunfire and two others were hit.

All these gunmen were "caught in the act." It was pretty plain that they had all acted alone, out of some insane desire for revenge or "justice."

The Kennedy killers were caught, too. But Oswald and Sirhan, unlike the others, may not have acted alone. They may have entered into conspiracies, plots that involved others. And nobody knows who these others might have been. The co-conspirators may have been kooks, like Oswald or Sirhan. On the other hand, they may have been government men, American or foreign, or other high-ranking figures.

That is why, in another sense, the Kennedy family has no right to stop the investigations. More may be at stake than the deaths of the two brothers, tragic as these losses were. The safety and security of the United States itself may be involved.

That is why many responsible people feel the search must go on.

Postscript:
Into the 1990's

Public interest in the assassinations of President John F. Kennedy and his brother U.S. Senator Robert F. Kennedy has never died down. People around the world want to know who killed the president and why and how he died. They also want to know more about the senator's killer, what the killer's hidden motives might have been, and whether he had acted alone. Their insistent questions led to the formation of the House Select Committee on Assassinations, a congressional group.

In 1978 the House Select Committee came to a conclusion that many private investigators had already reached: that the president's slaying was the result of a conspiracy. As we have already seen, a conspiracy means that two or more persons were involved in a criminal act.

Until that time, the Warren Commission's Report was the only official one. The report stated that a solitary gunman named Lee Harvey Oswald was responsible. Working alone, he shot and killed the president. Oswald was soon captured and held by the Dallas, Texas, police for two days. Then Oswald himself was slain as he was being transferred from one jail to another. Oswald's slayer was Jack Ruby.

The Warren Commission decided that Ruby acted for twisted emotional reasons and that he, too, acted alone. There was no conpiracy involved in either case. So said the Warren Commission.

The House Select Committee's declaration of conspiracy inspired a rash of books and at least two movies, as well as several TV programs. New ones keep popping up, well into the 1990's. Each book and movie has asserted that its analysis is the only foolproof one. As yet, however, none of these has been accepted as offering all the right answers.

Let's look at some of these accumulated ideas and theories, and perhaps come to some conclusions of our own. Bear in mind that some of these assertions and accusations sound highly believable. But remember, too, that no charges have been filed against anyone, and no arrests have been made. Will there be any in the future? Perhaps so; perhaps not.

The assassination data can be divided into three groups:

1. The Method, or Means: How was the president killed?

2. The Motives: Why was he killed?

3. The Men Involved: Who killed him?

1. *The Method, or Means.* While the president was riding in his open limousine, his back to the Texas School Book Depository, where, on the sixth floor, Oswald was said to have been perched. His rifle, propped up by book cartons, was aimed directly at the back of the president's head.

But ahead and to the right of the president's motorcade was the grassy knoll. There many spectators stood, ready to cheer the president as he passed by. Among them, another gunman may have been waiting for his chance to fire.

Oswald was accused of firing several shots from his position in the Texas School Book Depository. Two of these shots struck the president in the back of the head. But a third shot is said to have entered the president's throat, just above his Adam's apple, and emerged through the back of his neck.

Did this third shot actually go from the front of his neck to the back? Doctors at Parkland Hospital in Dallas, where the dying president was taken, and doctors at the Bethesda Naval Hospital near Washington, where the dead president was again examined, disagree. One group says there was an entry wound in his throat. The other group says there was an exit wound in his throat.

Many spectators standing on the grassy knoll at the time of the slaying reported hearing at least one rifle shot fired from nearby. They also reported seeing as many as four men hurrying away from the back of the knoll as soon as the shots were fired. The Warren investigators quizzed several of these witnesses but came to no conclusion.

Oswald may have indeed fired the shots that killed the president, but there is no clear-cut evidence that he alone did so. Nor was he even definitely linked with the sixth-floor window from where the shots were fired. Only minutes after the shooting, he was on the building's second floor, calmly drinking a Coca-Cola. Could he have left the firing site and cooled off so quickly? Here's another factor to consider: firing a cheap rifle, as Oswald did, should have left a powder burn on his cheek. After Oswald was arrested, his cheek was examined. No such powder burn was found.

After Oswald's death, his palm print was found on his rifle butt, indicating that it was he who did the shooting. Some investigators charge, however, that a palm print could have been transferred from his dead hand to the rifle butt. This could have been one of many illegal efforts to tie Oswald to the crime.

2. *The Motives*. Why was President Kennedy assassinated? Many reasonable speculations have been offered. None, however, has been positively proven.

One set of theories says that it was the president's plans for Vietnam that prompted his murder (see page 117). By 1963 (the assassination year), the United States was becoming more and more involved in the Vietnam war. The United States had already sent supplies, arms, and several thousand advisers and instuctors.

But the president wanted to go no further in aiding South Vietnam. He was ready to stop sending aid, even though South Vietnam claimed to have a democratic government and an army eager to wage war against North Vietnam. The president said that Vietnam was too far away from the United States, that South Vietnam's claim to democracy was false, and that the United States had no business sending American troops to fight in what was really a local war.

So, the theory goes, the president was killed by those who wanted the United States to become actively involved in the Vietnam war. Another theory holds that he was killed because he failed to help the Cuban exiles in their 1961 attempt to invade Cuba and overthrow the Communist govenment of Fidel Castro (see page 47). And still another theory claims that he did not destroy Cuba in the Cuban missile crisis of 1962 (see page 48), and so was slain.

Another theory involves the president's relationship with his brother when Robert Kennedy was attorney general. Robert was a relentless foe of organized crime. The only way to stop the attorney general was to kill the president. That's what some investigators think. They accuse the Mafia leaders and Jimmy Hoffa, the Teamster Union chief. Mind you, we are still talking theory. No real proof exists.

3. *The Men Involved:* The movie *JFK* was first shown in December, 1991, and will probably continue to be shown in theaters, on TV, and on videocassettes for years to come. The film screen credits acknowledge the help of two books: Jim Garrison's *On the Trail of the Assassins* and Jim Marrs's *Crossfire: The Plot That Killed Kennedy*.

The Garrison book is the partial autobiography of this former New Orleans district attorney. It is mainly about his struggle to convict a man named Clay Shaw for involvement in the Kennedy slaying. The book also tells of Shaw's friendship with Oswald during the 1963 summer in New Orleans. Garrison argues that Shaw's connection with Oswald makes him part of the Kennedy slaying.

Garrison's book ends with the not-guilty verdict that freed Clay Shaw. *On the Trail of the Assassins* is a true-to-life story, perhaps over-dramatized a bit when Garrison puts made-up words in his characters' mouths.

Marrs's book is factual, without a story line as in the Garrison book. It gathers up the accounts of many investigators, but comes to no binding conclusions.

The movie *JFK* is something else. It follows the story line of the Garrison book — up to a point, that is. The stunning conclusion abandons the cautious approach of the Garrison and Marrs books. Instead, it puts a direct, sweeping accusation in the mouth of a fictitious character known only as "X."

X proclaims that the conspiracy extends right up the the highest levels of the U.S. government — to the Pentagon, to the Joint Chiefs of Staff, to the FBI and the CIA, and to the White House itself.

The movie's director, producer, and writer are all one man, Oliver Stone. He is responsible for all these statements, and more. He goes on to tie in the military with American industry in a military/industrial alliance.

Stone does not name names. He says only that certain high-ranking men in these organizations were responsible for the death of the president. They wanted JFK killed because he was a threat to their plans. That's what Stone claims.

Stone's attack on major industries indicates a strong anti-Vietnam feeling. Industry wanted the Vietnam war to continue, he asserts — the more war, the higher industrial profits. It's as simple as that.

X's charge of conspiracy reaches up into the White House. Although X does not directly accuse by name the president who followed JFK into office, there can be no doubt that he meant President Lyndon B. Johnson, in office from 1963 to 1969. Johnson was Kennedy's vice president. Before that, he was the U.S. Senate's Majority Leader. He ran the Senate with an iron hand.

Kennedy had chosen Johnson as his running mate because Johnson could produce a winning number of votes. Johnson expected to take an active role in the Kennedy government. After entering office in 1961, however, he was largely ignored. His duties were mostly confined to cutting the ribbon when a new bridge or park was dedicated.

And Johnson was losing many of his once-loyal Texas followers. He sat silent, biding his time. That time came, his accusers say, when the president rode in the open limousine down a Dallas street. Johnson, his enemies claim, engineered the whole assassination program. And he took the presidential oath of office in Dallas only minutes after John F. Kennedy died.

These are extremely serious charges, but they cannot be proved. Investigators have not been able to link LBJ to the killing of JFK. Ambitious, yes, a powerful politician, yes, but an assassin, no. No way could he be linked to Oswald. (Another book, *The Texas Connection*, attempts to prove Johnson's guilt by eliminating all other suspects. Only Johnson is left. Therefore, he must be guilty, according to author Craig Zirbel.)

Clearly Oliver Stone was not sticking to the facts. In order to create a more dramatic film, he added his own fanciful ideas. If you see the movie, just remember to disbelieve certain parts of it.

As for Jack Ruby, Oswald's killer, new facts have come to life. Over the years it has been shown that he was a close associate of many criminals. They would have liked to see the president and his brother killed so that their illegal and unlawful activities could expand. But Ruby died, as we have seen, before he could tell his story.

Sirhan Sirhan, Robert Kennedy's slayer, remains securely locked up in a California prison. Every few years he petitions for a paroled release. Each time his petition is denied. It is not likely that he will ever win freedom. And he has not revealed any new facts about his crime.

SCHOLASTIC BIOGRAPHY

❏ MP44075-6	Bo Jackson: Playing the Games	$2.95
❏ MP42396-7	Christopher Columbus: Admiral of the Ocean Sea	$2.95
❏ MP45243-6	Colin Powell: A Biography	$2.95
❏ MP41836-X	Custer and Crazy Horse: A Story of Two Warriors	$2.95
❏ MP44570-7	The Death of Lincoln: A Picture History of the Assassination	$2.95
❏ MP45225-8	The Fairy Tale Life of Hans Christian Andersen	$2.75
❏ MP42218-9	Frederick Douglass Fights for Freedom	$2.50
❏ MP43628-7	Freedom Train: The Story of Harriet Tubman	$2.95
❏ MP43730-5	George Washington: The Man Who Would Not Be King	$2.75
❏ MP42402-5	Harry Houdini: Master of Magic	$2.50
❏ MP42404-1	Helen Keller	$2.50
❏ MP44652-5	Helen Keller's Teacher	$2.95
❏ MP44230-9	I Have a Dream: The Story of Martin Luther King	$2.75
❏ MP44336-4	Jennifer Capriati	$2.95
❏ MP42395-9	Jesse Jackson: A Biography	$2.75
❏ MP43503-5	Jim Abbott: Against All Odds	$2.75
❏ MP41344-9	John Fitzgerald Kennedy: America's 35th President	$2.50
❏ MP43827-1	The Life and Words of Martin Luther King, Jr.	$2.75
❏ MP41159-4	Lost Star: The Story of Amelia Earhart	$2.75
❏ MP44350-X	Louis Braille: The Boy Who Invented Books for the Blind	$2.75
❏ MP44154-X	Nelson Mandela "No Easy Walk to Freedom"	$2.95
❏ MP44144-2	New Kids in Town: Oral Histories of Immigrant Teens	$2.95
❏ MP42644-3	Our 41st President George Bush	$2.95
❏ MP43481-0	Pocahontas and the Strangers	$2.95
❏ MP41877-7	Ready, Aim, Fire! The Real Life Adventures of Annie Oakley	$2.75
❏ MP43052-1	The Secret Soldier: The Story of Deborah Sampson	$2.75
❏ MP44055-1	Squanto, Friend of the Pilgrims	$2.75
❏ MP42560-9	Stealing Home: The Story of Jackie Robinson	$2.95
❏ MP42660-5	The Story of George Washington Carver	$2.95
❏ MP42403-3	The Story of Thomas Alva Edison	$2.75
❏ MP45605-9	This Is David Robinson	$2.95
❏ MP42904-3	The Wright Brothers at Kitty Hawk	$2.95

Available wherever you buy books, or use this order form.

Scholastic Inc., P.O. Box 7502, 2931 East McCarty Street, Jefferson City, MO 65102

Please send me the books I have checked above. I am enclosing $_____ (please add $2.00 to cover shipping and handling). Send check or money order — no cash or C.O.D.s please.

Name _____

Address _____

City _____ State/Zip _____

Please allow four to six weeks for delivery. Available in the U.S. only. Sorry, mail orders are not available to residents of Canada. Prices subject to change.   BIO792